APUS & INCAS

A Cultural Walking & Trekking Guide to Cuzco Peru

Second Edition

Charles Brod

Inca Expeditions, Portland, Oregon

Edited by Karen Boush. Photos by Charles Brod
Drawings by David Swanson. Maps by Colleen Compton

Library of Congress Catalog Card Number: 88-838443
ISBN 0-9618296-1-3

Published by Inca Expeditions
2323 SE 46th Avenue
Portland, Oregon 97215

Distributed in Peru by Nuevas Imagenes
Av. Bolognesi 159
Lima 18, Peru

Cover photo: *Morning breaks over Nv. Ausangate in the Cordillera Vilcanota.*

In memory of Darlene Urfer,
whose love, understanding, and patience
helped teach her grandson
to read and write, and so much more.

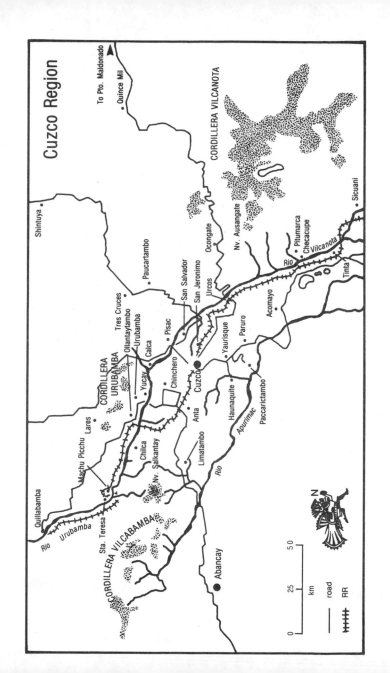

Cuzco Region

To Pto. Maldonado
• Quince Mil

CORDILLERA VILCANOTA

Shintuya •

• Paucartambo

Nv. Ausangate

Ocongate
•

Sicuani •

Tres Cruces
Ollantaytambo
Urubamba

San Salvador
San Jeronimo

Urcos

Pitumarca
Checacupe
Vilcanota
Rio

Tinta

CORDILLERA
URUBAMBA

• Pisac
Calca
Yucay

Chinchero

Yaurisque

Paruro

Acomayo

Machu Picchu   Lares

Chilca
Nv. Salkantay

Anta

Limatambo

Haunaquite

Apurimac

Paccarictambo

Quillabamba

Sta. Teresa

CORDILLERA VILCABAMBA

Rio   Urubamba

Rio

Cuzco

• Abancay

N

km
50   25   0

road
RR

Contents

Acknowledgments
Apus & Incas

Introduction to Walking & Trekking 1
   The Andes & Its People; Getting Ready; Health;
   Transportation; In the Country; Traditions & Beliefs

Day-Walks 37
   1. Plaza de Armas to the Ruins of Sacsayhuaman,
      Qenco, Puca Pucara, and Tambomachay 39
   2. Tambomachay to Pisac 43
   3. San Jeronimo to the Sanctuary of
      El Señor de Huanca 47
   4. Chinchero to the Sacred Valley by Inca Road 51
   5. Calca to the Ruins of Huchuy Qosqo 55
   6. Ollantaytambo to the Ruins of Pumamarca 59
   7. The Salt Ponds of Maras 63
   8. Cuzco to Paccarictambo 67

Treks 73
   1. The Inca Trail 75
   2. Chilca to Huayllabamba 87
   3. Ollantaytambo to Huayllabamba 93

The Cordillera Vilcabamba & Nv. Salkantay   97
    4. Mollepata to Huayllabamba   99
    5. Mollepata to Santa Teresa   109
    6. Mollepata to La Hidroelectrica   113

The Cordillera Vilcanota & Nv. Ausangate   117
    7. The Ausangate Circuit   119
    8. Tinqui to Pitumarca   129
    9. Pitumarca to Laguna Sibinacocha   133
   10. The Ausangate Short Circuit   143

The Cordillera Urubamba   145
   11. Ollantaytambo to Ccachin   151

Manu National Park   159

Appendix A
  Trilingual Guide   164

Appendix B
  The Legend of Inkarrí   167

Bibliography   168

Index   169

Acknowledgments

Standing atop a knoll with a stream's rushing waters far below, the tent faced toward the shimmering peak of Nv. Ausangate as a full moon rose behind my temporary home. Amid this idyllic setting the newly born idea of a hiking guidebook seemed like a brilliant endeavor. Since that cloudless night in May of 1985, the idea has at times faded; however, with people's support it has repeatedly regained the clarity of that first vision. It may sound trite but remains nonetheless true — without those people, this book would not have been possible.

During my stay in Cuzco to research the guidebook, many people aided me in my work and also strived to make this gringo feel at home. Tom Hendrickson of Peruvian Andean Treks often provided me with advice and invaluable trail information. The staff and teachers at the Excel Language Center not only offered me their sole typewriter, but gave to me constant encouragement, information, and bawdy companionship. In fact, from all the endless sessions of coffee drinking, long evenings of eating roasted chicken, and frenetic nights dancing at the disco, it was a wonder I managed to find any time or energy to hike and write. Most importantly, I would like to thank the Ciprian family and their relatives, who accepted me as part of their family and by so doing gave me a fuller understanding of the beauty and sadness of Peruvian life.

Over the short and hectic period that has brought this book into print, three people stand out in their commitment to the project. David Swanson with his enthusiasm and talent produced excellent drawings for the book. Colleen Compton created the maps for the book and also spent lunch hours and weekends with a calculator, papers, and drawings spread across a table, taking me step by step through the book designing and production process. Unfailing support was given to me by Karen Boush throughout the entire project. Her words of encouragement often comforted me, and her instructive comments, questions and deft editing of the text combined to thwart lurking errors and to create a readable, understandable guide.

I owe all these people deep appreciation and thanks for what they have done for me.

Charles Brod
Portland, Oregon
May, 1986

APUS & INCAS

Introduction to
Walking & Trekking

The Andes & Its People

Throughout the Andean mountain range, interconnecting paths create a trail system of sierra intersections and valley thoroughfares. Wander to one mountain top, and you'll find a deep valley opening below you, its sides laced with waterfalls and its crest crowned by snowcapped peaks. Walk through a village of thatched-roof houses, and you'll feel as though you've taken a step back in time. Turn a bend, and you'll catch glimpses of wildlife found nowhere else in the world. The powerful magnetism of the Andes will soon have you wanting to explore farther afield, beyond the relative comforts of town and the roadside ruins. No better place exists for this than Cuzco, Peru. The rural countryside and its inhabitants offer the South American traveler true contact with the beauty and culture of the Andes.

Geography. In geological terms, the Andes are considered to be relatively young mountains. They were formed some fifty to sixty million years ago, during the early Tertiary period of the Cenozoic era, when the Earth's crust buckled diastrophically and created a great ridge on the east and a submarine trough on the west. As a result, the Earth's surface rises from 6100 meters below sea level to 6100 meters above sea level, at some points in just the small span of 320 kilometers (200 miles).

The movement formed the world's second-highest mountain chain. More than seventy-five Andean mountain peaks measure above 6100 meters (20,000 feet) high, and some two thousand more reach above 4875 meters (16,000 feet) high. Only the Himalayas surpass the Andes in height; the Andes do, however, form the longest continuous chain of mountains in the world, stretching 6440 kilometers (over 4000 miles) from the Cordillera Santa Maria mountains in Colombia to the Tierra del Fuego at the southern tip of Chile. They would continue even farther south had not a length of the mountains receded into the ocean, isolating the Palmer peninsula of Antarctica from the South American continent. The width of the ranges varies: in Ecuador they measure only some 100 kilometers (60 miles) wide, while in Bolivia their width extends to over 300 kilometers (180 miles).

The earth's buckling not only formed one of the world's highest mountain chains, but it also created the frigid Humboldt Current of the Pacific. Partly because of this current, the Pacific coastal plain alongside the Andes is a 3200-kilometer-long (2000-mile) desert, one of the world's driest. The temperature inversions of the current permit only a small amount of rain to fall on the coast. Equally unexpected as the dry land itself is the gray mist, called *garúa,* that wraps much of the desert coastside from March to November. The garúa neither condenses into rain nor burns off under the sun's heat. Instead, it lingers, encasing the land in a damp mantle that shadows and obscures the horizon.

South America's continental divide runs, on the average, only 100 kilometers (60 miles) from the Pacific coast, yet most rivers of the Andes do not run to the Pacific. They drain to the Atlantic, some 4800 kilometers (3000 miles) to the east. These rivers, plenishing the jungle that lies to the east of the Andes, join to form the greatest river system in the world, the Amazon

Basin. In harsh contrast, the western coastal land is only occasionally broken by the oasis of a river valley.

Cuzco. The ancient city of Cuzco, the capital of the southern Peruvian department of the same name, was built across the upper end of a trough-shaped valley. Bordered by the rio Vilcanota/Urubamba and the rio Apurimac, the Cuzco valley runs southeast, connecting with a number of other valleys that lead to the 4318-meter-high gap at La Raya. Southeast of La Raya, the high, desolate plain of the Altiplano spreads out around Lake Titicaca and into Bolivia.

Three major mountain ranges rise up near Cuzco. To Cuzco's northwest stand the mountains of the Cordillera Vilcabamba, its highest peak being Nevado Salkantay, at 6271 meters (20,574 feet). To the city's southeast rises the Cordillera Vilcanota, with the 6372-meter-high (20,905-foot) Nevado Ausangate towering above its surroundings. To the north of Cuzco stands the Cordillera Urubamba, with the peaks of Pitusiray, Chicon, Helancoma, and Veronica overlooking the Sacred Valley of the Incas.

Cuzco's location makes some of the best hiking in the world easily accessible. Many of the day-walks outlined in the book have their starts or finishes in the Sacred Valley. This valley cuts through the heart of the once-vast Inca empire, and it is rich in ruins and trails leading to them. Each mountain range, though geographically close to its lofty neighbors, maintains particular environmental and cultural differences. This variety of scenery and people, combined with the unique history of the area, make trekking and walking outside of Cuzco a true adventure.

History. The grandeur of the mountains that surround Cuzco is equaled only by that of the many Indian cultures that have influenced and left their marks on the region. The artifacts, ruins, legends, beliefs, and superstitions that were left behind by pre-Columbian cultures contribute to the character of the Andes as much as the majestic mountains themselves.

Man had first come to the Americas from Asia, crossing the Bering Strait to colonize North America during the Paleolithic period, estimated around 25,000 B.C. By 10,000 B.C., they had migrated to South America and were inhabiting the Andes. Archaeological studies have reached back to 7000 B.C. in deciphering the earliest remains of man found in the region.

Several great Indian cultures flourished in Peru prior to the Inca empire. Between approximately 900 B.C. and 1438 A.D., the Chavin, Tiahuanaco, Mochica, and Chimor kingdoms subsequently established themselves. Because no written language existed in pre-Columbian South America, the existences of these cultures are recorded only by artifacts — such items as finely crafted pottery, precious metal ornaments, intricately woven textiles, and impressively carved stone.

Visitors to the Andes, however, seem to find the remnants of the final pre-Columbian culture — the Incas — the most entrancing. The Incas, the last great civilization to be discovered and conquered by the Europeans, ruled an empire that stretched over 3500 kilometers (2200 miles) long, reaching as far north as present-day Pasto, Colombia, and as far south as the rio Maule in Chile. The empire was narrow, however; confined by the Pacific coast on the west, it crossed the Andes but stopped at the eastern edge of the mountains, measuring an average of 320 kilometers (200 miles) in width. In total, the Incas controlled an empire comparable to that of the Romans. They are renowned for their engineering feats and their ability to maintain order while still providing food and clothing for their subjects — all with a Bronze Age technology that did not include the aid of the wheel. This vast empire, built up in the brief period of a hundred and fifty years, came to a sudden end when Francisco Pizarro and his hundred and fifty conquistadores arrived in 1532.

The name Andes originated with the Incas, but it did not denote the mountains we think of today. Andes derived from the Quechua word *anti*, which during the Inca empire referred to only the mountains east of Cuzco. Quechua, the language of the Incas, is still used today by Indians in many areas of Peru, Bolivia, and Ecuador. Various interpretations of the word exist, but Garcilaso de la Vega, a chronicler who was born shortly after the Conquest and who was half Inca himself, attributed the name to a tribe east of Cuzco. When the Spanish arrived in the sixteenth century, they applied *Ande* to the entire mountainous region.

The last Incas died hundreds of years ago, but they left behind an impressive array of monuments by which to remember them. Amazing as these ruins are, they form only the most apparent vestige of a lost civilization. Ancient beliefs, traditions, and customs live on, hidden in the hearts, minds, and daily lives of the Quechua people. You need only explore their highland home to glimpse a culture that has survived brutal conquest to struggle on through the centuries.

Getting Ready

Weather. One of the most important aspects of planning your trip is to anticipate what the weather will be like. The trail, your equipment, and even your food will all be affected by the moods of the sky.

Since Peru lies in the Southern Hemisphere, one would naturally expect the seasons of the year there to be opposite those of the North. Technically speaking, they are opposite, but practically speaking, the winters of the Peruvian Andes are clear and dry, and the summers cloudy and wet.

In this region of the world, the terms winter, spring, summer, and fall do not apply because there are actually only two seasons: the rainy season, from October to April, and the dry season, from May to September. During the rainy season in Cuzco, the afternoons are filled with intense downpours. In the dry season, the skies remain clear and the air cold. Recent years, however, have proved these weather patterns less reliable than in the past.

The mean temperature in Cuzco hovers at 12 degrees Celsius, though evening temperatures often fall below freezing during the dry season. Of course, out in the mountains as altitude is gained there is a corresponding drop in temperature. In the rarefied air of the Andes, the intense rays of the sun can burn you in just a few minutes. Step into a shady spot, however, and you find yourself chilled and shivering.

The regular hiking season runs from May through September, with peak activity occurring in the coldest months of June, July, and August. My personal preference is to hike in April and May, when the temperatures are less extreme and the countryside has not yet been scorched to a drab and dusty brown. In the rainy season, trails can become rivers of mud, so it is often best to check with local outfitters on area conditions before setting out during this season. Though no matter what the season, you should be ready for all types of weather conditions.

Equipment. You will find it to be true that the better the equipment you take with you on the trail, the more enjoyable your hike will be. But do not allow inadequate gear or a lack of equipment to deter you from trekking or walking. For while in Peru, do as the Peruvians do, and that means making do with whatever is available.

Day-walks. Your needs are relatively small for day-walks. A good pair of walking boots or shoes is the most important item on your list. Tennis shoes will do in a pinch, though they often do not provide the best possible traction. Also, depending on the season, be sure to take either sun or rain gear, or both.

to snow. By late afternoon, the snow and rain had stopped. Before turning in that night, clear skies once again opened above me to reveal the stars and moon. Be prepared!

Outfitters. If you find yourself lacking some of the most basic equipment, there are a number of agencies that rent gear. Check the gear for fit and wear before leaving the shop. Often the equipment is not in the best of condition. The following agencies will be happy to rent equipment and provide trail information.

Inca Treks
Procuradores 345, Of.1
Tel. 232594

Snow Tours
Procuradores 347
Tel. 241313

Walking Travel
Portal Confituria 265, Of. 3
Plaza de Armas
Tel. 223049

Orquideas Tours
Portal Comercio 141
Plaza de Armas
Tel. 231515

Veronica Tours
Marquez 215
Tel. 231565

Explorandes
Procuradores 372

Packs for both trekking and day walks can be bought either at Leon Sport, Centro Commercial Ollanta, Av. Sol 344; or at Campo, Calle Suecia 328. If you are looking to put together an impromptu adventure, whether it be in the mountains, on the river, or in the jungle, try the Adventure Center at Procuradores 50. They provide equipment, guides, logistical support, and information on a variety of outdoor activities.

Pack animals. Pack horses and their handlers, *arrieros,* can be arranged for at Tinqui and Mollepata for trips respectively to Nevados Ausangate and Salkantay. Prices vary, but a horse can be hired for a day for approximately one to one and a half American dollars, with the arriero receiving an equal amount.

Although it is not obligatory, you should consider taking extra food for the arriero.

Food. Packing food for a trek requires more planning than packing food for a day-hike. You should estimate the number of days you plan to hike, then pack accordingly, supplementing what you've packed with a couple more days' worth of food. This will ensure that you do not run out of food in case of unexpected trouble. It also gives you the option of prolonging your hike if you want to.

I have encountered two types of hikers. One likes to eat heartily on the trail, the food being as much a part of the hike as the scenery. The other enjoys traveling light. Food, though necessary, is viewed by this type of hiker as more of a burden than a boon. How much and what a hiker will eat depends on his or her own personal preferences and needs.

Your first decision in preparing your larder must be whether or not you will take a stove. Little or no firewood is available along most of the routes described, so a stove is a necessity if you want hot food. Stoves can be rented from the agencies listed previously, or a bulky kerosene-burning model can be purchased in the San Pedro market. If you have a stove that uses white gas, *bencina,* try the *ferreterias,* Peruvian hardware stores, around the market or in Limacpampa at the beginning of Av. de la Cultura.

The easiest and perhaps most interesting place to do your shopping is in the main market across from the San Pedro train station. Here you can find almost all the items you need. Otherwise, you can do your shopping in the small shops or one of the supermarkets located in the Plaza de Armas, on Av. Sol, or on Calle Matara. Do not plan on buying food in the small towns at the start of hikes. Their shops are high-priced and stocked with only the most basic items.

The following list contains items readily available in Cuzco.

Items not requiring cooking
 1. Bread — *pan*
 2. Cheese — *queso*
 3. Salt/pepper — *sal/pimiento*
 4. Canned tuna/sardines — *atun/sardines en lata*
 5. Hard-boiled eggs — *huevos pasados*
 6. Candy/chocolate — *dulces/chocolate*
 7. Crackers — *galletas*
 8. Dried fruit/nuts — *secas/nueces*
 9. Marmalade — *mermelade*
10. Oatmeal — *avena*
11. Sugar — *azucar*
12. Cocoa — *cacao*
13. Powdered milk — *leche en polvo*

The last six items on the list can be combined with cold or hot water to make a filling and not-completely unappetizing porridge.

Items requiring cooking
1. Instant coffee/tea — *cafe/te*
2. Eggs — *huevos*
3. Packet soups — *sopas*
4. Noodles — *fideos*
5. Tomato paste — *pasta de tomate*
6. Spices — *especias*

Some final recommendations: Solid marmalade is best because it will not leak and leave a mess. Buy the packaged oatmeal since most of the bulk type is best used for animal fodder. Delicious cheeses are sold in the San Pedro market, and the bread from the Govinda Restaurant is a personal favorite of mine.

Maps. Maps have been included for all the treks and day walks outlined in this book. The greatest effort has been made to ensure their accuracy. You may wish, however, to supplement these maps with others that provide greater detail on the vast regions covered.

Maps of the Cuzco region vary widely in their quality and accuracy. A number of Inca Trail maps that differ in style and quality can be found in Cuzco, but if you are looking for maps of other areas, it is best to plan ahead and go to the *Instituto Geografico Militar,* located at Av. Aramburu 1190 in Lima. Here they are happy to sell you whatever maps they have available.

The IGM supplies topographic maps that have a scale of 1:100,000 (1cm = 1km) for the Cuzco area, the Calca (Sacred Valley) region, and the Ocongate (Ausangate) region. The maps, with places often misnamed, trails indicated where there are no trails, and vice versa, are not completely accurate.

The IGM's maps for the area around Machu Picchu and Salkantay are of a lesser quality. A map in a 1:200,000 scale entitled "Anta" includes Ollantaytambo, Chinchero, and the area between Mollepata and Salkantay. An even worse map for the Salkantay area is also in a 1:200,000 scale and was produced in the 1950s. Entitled "Cuzco Norte," the map resembles a blueprint with distorted distances and topographic lines blurred into unintelligible mountains and valleys. Needless to say, this map is difficult to read but may soon be replaced by others.

South American Explorers Club. This non-profit organization, which has offices in Lima and in Denver, Colorado, is a valuable resource for travel and trail information. Founded in 1977, the club supports scientific field exploration and research, promotes adventure sports, facilitates the exchange of scientific and travel information on South America, and works for wilderness and wildlife preservation. Membership to the organization costs $25 a year, helps to support these noble causes, and gets you a subscription to their quarterly publication, plus discounts on books, maps (SAEC maps of both the Inca Trail and the Ausangate region are available), and other paraphernalia for sale by the club. Members may also use the clubhouse in Lima for storage during their travels. Nonmembers may avail themselves of the club's books and information, but not at discount prices. The Lima clubhouse will take hiking and camping equipment on consignment, but they do not purchase gear outright.

In Lima the clubhouse is located at Av. Portual 146 (Brena), next to the prison and a few blocks from the U.S. Embassy. The mailing address is Casilla 3714, Lima 100, Peru (Tel: 314480). The U.S. office is located at 1510 York Street, Denver, CO 80206 (Tel: 303-320-0388).

How to use this book. No book should require a lengthy explanation on how it should be read, but a few explanations and clarifications may prevent undue confusion and misunderstanding. General trail information, which I have attempted to make as accurate as possible given the sources available, is provided at the beginning of each walk and trek. "Elevation gain" and "Elevation loss" refer to the amount of elevation gained from the trail's starting point to its highest point, and elevation lost from its highest point to its end point. This is true for all the trails except the Cuzco-to-Paccarictambo hike, where the trail ends at an elevation higher than its lowest point. Trail distance is given in kilometers and is my own best estimate of the distance between a trail's start and finish. Hence, these distances are a matter of judgment and not completely reliable. "Length" refers to the amount of time an average hiker should need to cover the trail, not including time needed for transport to the trailhead.

In each trek section, I have included walking times between major points along the trail. I have tried to remain consistent throughout the book so that individual hikers can gauge their pace against the book's and get an accurate idea of a trail's length. The compass directions are based on magnetic readings.

I have strived to retain the local flavor of place names by using the Spanish designations — *rio* for river and *nevado* (Nv.) for mountain. Other foreign words are *puna,* meaning a highland grassy area, and *pampa,* meaning pasture. The most difficult term to define is *quebrada.* Quebrada denotes both a stream and the narrow, steep valley that it flows through, but it translates most closely to a ravine with a stream.

One final geographic note: In the Sacred Valley of the Incas you can find the rios Vilcanota and Urubamba. Although the waters remain the same, the river's name changes halfway down the valley. The Vilcanota flows from the mountain range of the same name but at a point between the towns of Calca and Urubamba becomes the Urubamba. I refer to this single river by both names, my choice depending on what part of the valley I am describing.

Throughout the walking and trekking sections, I've used the metric system, as is the custom in South America. To avoid needless math anxiety, conversion tables are provided below.

1 kg = 2.2 lbs.	500 m = 1,640 ft.	5 km = 3.1 miles
1 cm = .4 inches	1,000 m = 3,280 ft.	10 km = 6.2 miles
1 m = 3.28 ft.	3,000 m = 9,840 ft.	20 km = 12.4 miles
1 ft. = .3 m	4,000 m = 13,120 ft.	30 km = 18.6 miles
1 km = ⅝ mile	5,000 m = 16,400 ft.	40 km = 24.8 miles
1 mile = 1.6 km	6,000 m = 19,680 ft.	60 km = 37.3 miles

The formulae for temperature conversions between Fahrenheit and Celsius:

$$(1.8 \times °C) + 32° = °F$$
$$(°F - 32) \div 1.8 = °C$$

Health

Ensure good health during your visit by taking preventive measures before traveling to South America. Immunize yourself against polio, measles, typhoid, yellow fever, tetanus, and diphtheria. Though not 100 percent effective, a gamma globulin shot to deter hepatitis may give you a preventive edge. Consult a doctor as to the proper sequence of these shots several months in advance of your departure date. If you are traveling into malarial regions of the jungle, you will also want to take a sequence of anti-malaria pills.

Cuzco lies at 3,400 meters (11,150 feet) above sea level. If the city is your first high-altitude stop, you may feel the effects of high-altitude sickness. You will gradually adjust, however, to the altitude through acclimatization, a process where your body compensates for the reduced oxygen level in the air and for the lower air pressure of high altitude, both of which affect the rate of oxygen transfer to the lungs.

Your system acclimatizes by producing additional red blood cells that contain more oxygen-carrying hemoglobin. A 2.3 percent increase in red blood cells occurs with every 915 meters (3,000 feet) of altitude gained. So if you come to Cuzco from sea level, your red-blood-cell count will increase approximately 8.5 percent to acclimatize to the higher altitude. Also, the surface of the lungs increases, facilitating a greater transfer of oxygen to the blood stream.

Acclimatization can take approximately six weeks to occur fully, but after several days you should feel comfortable enough to perform moderate activity. You are acclimatizing when headaches, dizziness, and lightheadedness subside, and when appetite improves and sleep becomes easier. On arrival, the best plan to follow is to take it easy the first few days. Spend time visiting the local ruins and Sacred Valley rather than embarking on any trek. Try an easy day-walk, such

s the tour of the ruins above Cuzco, or the hike from Ollantaytambo to the ruins of Pumamarca.

A simple way of avoiding altitude sickness while hiking is to pace yourself. Do not overexert yourself when climbing hills and passes. Instead, try to synchronize your breathing with your steps. Through conscious effort you can avoid over-stressing your respiratory system, making hiking easier and probably helping increase your stamina.

High-Altitude Sickness. There are three types of altitude sickness; their effects range from mild discomfort to death. When in the mountains, it is important to be on the lookout for the early warning signs and to act accordingly.

The most common form of altitude sickness is Acute Mountain Sickness (AMS), also known as *soroche.* Symptoms of AMS are loss of appetite, headaches, nausea, dizziness, breathlessness, insomnia, weakness, and a higher pulse rate. In advanced cases, there can be severe vomiting, a complete loss of appetite, lassitude, loss of coordination, and a reduced volume of urine.

The local remedy for AMS is coca tea, but the curative powers of the drink are rather limited. For mild cases, modern medicine has provided several drugs. Diamox, a mild diuretic that can alleviate and even prevent the primary symptoms of AMS, is available in the United States with a doctor's prescription. It is sometimes sold in Cuzco, but more readily available in this city is the drug Coramina, which increases blood circulation.

To prevent AMS, drink plenty of liquids, avoid overexertion, and stick to a high-carbohydrate diet. Most importantly, a graded ascent will give your body time to adjust. Never sleep more than 300 meters higher than your previous night's camp. Also, it is best to hike a little higher each day than the night's sleeping altitude.

Pulmonary Edema (PE) is one of the severe, possibly fatal, forms of altitude sickness. The lungs of a PE victim fill with fluids until he or she literally drowns. PE's fatal process occurs quickly and with few warning signs, so a fellow hiker's alertness can be a lifesaving factor.

The primary signs of PE are the same as AMS, but are also accompanied by an incessant cough, which remains dry until an advanced stage, when white or pink sputum is coughed up. With each breath, there is a rattling sound in the chest, and the victim may also feel a tightness there. Other possible symptoms are blue-gray fingernails and lips, and rapid breathing and heartbeat. Lassitude is sometimes the only early symptom. PE progresses rapidly, with the onset of primary symptoms occurring in the first or second day upon reaching altitude. It is then only another one or two days before PE reaches a critical stage.

Detected early, PE can be treated with a short descent of 300 to 500 meters, followed by rest. Otherwise, in more severe cases, or if the patient doesn't respond at the lower altitude, an immediate descent to a significantly lower altitude is the only cure. Oxygen can be administered, but is not a cure.

Cerebral Edema (CE) is another high-altitude killer. Fluid collects in the brain, causing brain damage or death. The symptoms of CE are much the same as AMS, along with confusion, a loss of energy and interest in anything, hallucinations, and a lack of coordination. Again, the only cure for CE is immediate evacuation to a lower altitude.

Remember, people suffering from altitude sickness can lose their judgment. It is important that hiking companions be alert and take decisive action. When evacuating a stricken companion, use a stretcher, because walking will only speed the deadly process. Transporting a victim on horseback is also dangerous. Loss of balance is a common factor in altitude sickness, and a fall will only complicate matters.

Hypothermia. Also known as exposure, hypothermia is the rapid loss of body heat with the body unable to generate sufficient warmth to replace what is lost. It is unlikely that you will experience such extreme cold in the Cuzco area to place you in danger of hypothermia, but cold temperatures are not the only causes of hypothermia. Usually, the body needs only to become wet in windy and moderately cold conditions for the process to set in.

The first sign of hypothermia is uncontrollable shivering. The shivering will then stop, but the body remains cold. When the body temperature has been lowered sufficiently, the victim becomes drowsy and may even feel warm. Dropping off into unconsciousness, the victim is only a short way from death.

The best way to prevent hypothermia is by staying warm and dry. Change your clothes when they become wet. Have a tent that will provide proper shelter from wind and rain, and set it up in a protected area.

If a companion shows signs of hypothermia, set up camp immediately. A too-rapid evacuation may lead to shock. Dry the victim off, put him in a sleeping bag, and since his body is not generating heat, use your own naked body to supply heat to his. Also, if possible, feed him hot liquids in small quantities.

Sunstroke. The rays of the sun are made more intense in the Andes due to the thin atmosphere of high altitudes. Sunstroke, also known as heat exhaustion, can happen here even though the temperatures are not extreme. In the dry Andean air, the body can lose moisture and become dehydrated.

Symptoms of sunstroke are a rapid heartbeat, nausea, dizziness, headaches, and even loss of consciousness. Although not a serious condition, sunstroke can be debilitating. The best way to prevent and cure sunstroke is to drink plenty of liquids with an ample amount of salt, protect yourself from the sun with hat and clothing, and rest in the shade.

Water. It is best to sterilize water while on the trail with either tablets or boiling. The problem with boiling is that if you boil all the water you drink, you will need a tanker truck to carry sufficient stove fuel. A tincture of iodine solution *(tinquier de yodo)* will kill just about everything in water except hepatitis. Three drops should be adequate to sterilize a liter of water.

Drinking untreated water is a gamble. There have been cases of giardiasis reported along the Inca Trail. Nevertheless, you will be tempted by the mountain streams. In the upper regions, away from the pastures and villages, the cascading mountain water is relatively safe to drink untreated.

Although you might not notice it, the altitude and sun cause rapid dehydration. Drink out of habit, not out of thirst. Each person should carry at least two liters of water. Under moderate exertion and clear skies, a person should drink a liter of water every few hours. Always keep a good supply of water on hand. Whenever I disobeyed this rule, I regretted it.

Transportation

It is said that getting there is half the fun. This truism may be pushed to its limits when you are crammed into the hard, straight-backed seat of a train with a baby crying in your face and with a man who has neither shaved in days nor bathed in an even remoter time falling asleep on your shoulder. These are the times when you should try and keep your sense of adventure.

Trucks and trains are about the only practical way of getting around the Cuzco region. They serve all areas lying within a day's journey by road or rail of Cuzco. Of course, depending on your budget and destination, a taxi may also be hired. Hitchhiking is not an option in Peru, since there is no tradition of thumbing a ride. If you are picked up at the roadside, you will most likely be expected to pay.

Cuzco has two train stations; both are run by Enafer, the state-owned railroad. The San Pedro terminal is located across from the central market and serves the area north of Cuzco, including Ollantaytambo, Chilca, Km 88, Machu Picchu, and Quillabamba. The local train leaves twice a day — once in the early morning and again in the afternoon — and makes numerous stops along the route. The tourist train, though much more elegant and expensive, makes an almost-nonstop run to Machu Picchu. The Huanchac terminal, located near the end of Av. Sol on Av. Pachacutec, serves the towns southeast of Cuzco, including those located to the west of Nv. Ausangate. Local trains only go as far as Sicuani, but the daily train to Puno and Lake Titicaca also leaves from this terminal.

It is best to buy your tickets in advance. Train tickets normally go on sale at both terminals a half-day prior to departure. For example, if you want to ride the morning local to Km 88, buy your ticket the afternoon before the train leaves.

All remote towns located on roads are served by trucks. The problem is finding out where and when the trucks leave Cuzco for these destinations. With enough asking around, you will find that secret place and time. Towns at the foothills of Nevados Salkantay and Ausangate are served by regular truck transport, the only way of reaching these mountain areas. The appropriate trek sections give specific departure information for these two areas.

Sacred Valley. Minibuses into the Sacred Valley depart daily at frequent intervals from just before sunrise to just after sunset. Buses for Pisac and Calca leave from Av. Tacna between Av. de la Cultura and Av. Garcilaso. Buses direct to Urubamba leave from Av. Huascar 128 just above Mercado Huanchac. If you want to get to Ollantaytambo, you'll need to take a small truck or van from Urubamba.

Travel by truck is often the only transport to trailheads.

Although it is no problem getting to the valley, problems can arise on your return to Cuzco in the late afternoon. The push-and-shove race for the last available space on vans out of the valley can be maddening. On weekends the seat grab can be particularly frantic. Just to be safe, give yourself a few hours before sunset to get out of the valley.

Trucks. When taking any truck, keep a few things in mind. Truck drivers are notorious for overcharging passengers — gringos and locals alike. One way to prevent price-gouging is to watch to see what others are paying. If this is not possible, ask a fellow passenger what the normal fare is. If you and your companions are to be the only passengers transported in the vehicle, agree on a price before setting out. Otherwise, you may be in for a surprise when you get out to pay.

Also, you should keep an eye on your backpack. This is not so much because of theft, but because of possible mistreatment. The back of trucks are commonly crowded, cramped places where passengers sit on their shapeless bundles. To prevent your backpack from being stepped on, buried under sacks of onions, or stained by leaky kerosene jugs, find a place out of harm's way — if such a place exists.

You yourself will undergo the same perils as your gear, but with a great deal more discomfort for you than for your inanimate baggage. Space is at a premium and what little space you have will most likely be encroached upon. Polite behavior does not apply in these situations. If you are pushed against, do not hesitate to push back. If someone dangles their feet in your face, complain. If that doesn't remove them from your sight, knock them away. Such physical jostling offends no one and is all part of the ride.

One particular notorious ride sticks in my memory. I was returning from Paccarictambo. I chose to ride in a small pickup. Ten people in the back were needed to start. This, however, did not preclude our picking up more passengers along the way.

Sharing the back of this truck with nine others, I had found enough space at the rear to get all of my 6-foot frame in the bed. All of it, that is, except for one leg that I dangled over the back. The driver repeatedly scolded me for my errant leg, then laughed at my discomfort. There must be a Peruvian law of the road which states that a vehicle is not overloaded until limbs begin to lop over the sides. Each time I was reprimanded, I would place my offending leg in the truck, and wait until the driver returned to the cab before I once again stretched it out to rest on the bumper.

Along the way, I quickly learned why the rear of the truck was an unpopular riding spot. The wheels, speeding over an unpaved road, kicked up a great deal of dust, the vast majority of which circulated up and over the tailgate to deposit itself in my right ear.

We soon stopped to pick up a woman who, finding room

nowhere else in the truck, made some next to me. She carried with her a piglet wrapped in a burlap bag. While she settled into the truck, the piglet made quite evident his feelings about the accommodations by squealing in my one unclogged ear. As the truck started to move, the piglet's snout, protruding from a hole in the sack, eagerly snuffled the air and probed whatever he could find. One of the things he happened to discover was the region of my thighs and crotch. To let Porky know that his personal probings were not appreciated in the least, I abruptly pushed the flat of my hand against the flat of his nose. The pig gave out an offended snort, and I believe the woman called me a brute in Quechua. Things settled down and I was finally able to endure the ride in relative peace and discomfort.

Determining the departure time of a truck can be as frustrating as the ride can be uncomfortable. The driver's reassurance that the truck will be leaving *muy pronto* — very soon — can mean you might not be on your way for a couple more hours. Economics dictate that a truck will not leave for its destination until it is crammed full or crammed near-full. Even then, after the truck has started and is moving, this does not necessarily mean that you are on your way. The driver will spend more time driving around nearby streets in hopes of finding just a couple more passengers. Then, he'll stop for gas. And finally, once you're out on the open road, don't be surprised if the truck breaks down, or if a boy is sent scurrying down a hillside to retrieve water from a stream for the radiator. Getting there might not be fun, but it certainly can be maddening.

Trains. Trains are equally as uncomfortable as trucks, but for different reasons. The aged trains are more often than not late to their destinations. On sunny days, the cars can feel like ovens. By mid-journey, aisles are littered with pop bottles that roll about the floor and make random contact with floorboards, seats, and feet. Although I have never been sick on a train, I have often sat next to people who are. Usually a window is available, but sometimes one is not.

Robbery on the trains is a constant problem. The local train to Machu Picchu and Quillabamba has become notorious for camera and bag snatching. The best way to guard against this happening to you is to watch your gear, secure it to the luggage rack, or hold it against your body. You are most vulnerable during the confusion and crowding that occurs at stops and in stations. Thieves often work by a method of distraction. Your attention is diverted only momentarily, yet the next thing you know your possessions are gone. You needn't be paranoid, just alert, and you won't be robbed.

In the Country

The Cuzco region can truly be a hiker's paradise. Luckily for him or her, it is not a siren's song leading to unexpected perils. The climate is a mild one, the trails are visible, if not well-worn, and the mountain inhabitants are, for the most part, friendly to outsiders. The mountains can be a relatively safe and hospitable environment — if you follow a few basic rules and take some precautions.

Trails. The trails detailed in this book are easily followed and offer no great dangers in normal conditions. At times a trail will split and run in two or more plausible directions. As a general rule, take the wider, well-worn path. If the trail runs out or seems to lead in the wrong direction, turn back and start again. Don't push ahead; you will only get yourself in trouble.

If the weather turns bad, obscuring the trail or making footing difficult, stop and wait until conditions improve. This is particularly valid on and near mountain passes, where trails are often the most precarious.

On my first hike past Nv. Ausangate, I was just approaching the mountain when a thick hail began to fall. I took shelter in a hut, where I stayed until its occupants returned and I, lacking a command of Quechua, had to excuse myself as best I could. The hail had let up a little by then, so I decided to continue on my way. It was a brief reprieve, however, and soon the hail was falling as hard as ever. As I ascended, the trail's visibility actually increased as the path turned into a smooth, flat line blanketed by the hailstones.

Trouble came when I began my descent. The trail resembled nothing more than a slick rut in the mountainside, a thin line of footing between me and a long, rough slide to the valley floor far below. Now, with the sun falling behind the mountains to the northwest, I weighed my prospects — falling into the valley or spending a night huddled against the muddy mountainside. Liking neither option, I gathered enough courage to squirm and shuffle my way down the trail to more level ground, spending the night shaken but wiser.

Robbery. Theft along most of the trails described in this book is infrequent. However, an influx of gringos and their accompanying goodies into remote areas can provide an overwhelming temptation to a few local inhabitants. To ensure that a gringo and his goodies are not soon parted, you should take a few general precautions.

The most effective way to prevent casual theft of your gear is to keep it in your tent and your tent closed. You should do this whenever you are away from your tent, no matter for how short a time. If it is impractical to keep gear in the tent while you are sleeping, either hide it next to the tent or, my favorite unproved foil, secure the straps of the backpack to the tent and cover it in noisy plastic.

Theft along the Inca Trail is the exception to the rule. It has become a persistent problem. Along with the increasing popularity of the trail, so has there been an increase in robbery, from nighttime camp thieving to daylight armed robbery. Periodic police sweeps along the Inca Trail do curtail the robberies, but the captured robbers are soon replaced by new criminals. Full-time patrols along the trail have been talked about for some time now, but no concrete action has been taken.

Traveling in a large group is one recommended safeguard when walking the trail. There have been reports, however, of groups with as many as seven members held at gunpoint and robbed of their gear. Another report tells of a group of four who were left with nothing but the underwear they had on. Nonetheless, traveling in a large group may deter the less ambitious robber.

Campesinos, meaning "farmers," is currently the official word used to denote Peru's Indian population, which makes up 40 percent of the country's twenty million inhabitants. Calling a person *indio,* Indian, is a terrible insult, the word carrying negative connotations of backwardness and stupidity, a stigma that hangs upon Peru's lowest class no matter what word defines it.

The campesinos of the highlands are generally good people who rarely give hikers problems. They will laugh at you and call you gringo (it is not an insult), but otherwise leave you alone. They can be very generous in their giving of food and drink. The worst treatment I ever received from a campesino was in fact a gesture of friendship from an old man who carried with him a jug of *cañaso,* the Peruvian version of white lightning. We met on a trail as I descended and he ascended. He liberally mixed his Spanish and Quechua, with a great deal more emphasis on the latter. I just nodded and threw in an occasional *sí-sí.* He then offered me a shot from his jug. Thinking it to be just a weak spirit, I took the grimy capful of clear liquor and quickly swallowed it. I have never tasted such vile liquid before or after. The expression on my face must have been quite comic, but my companion was too busy talking and filling another cap to notice. When I was offered the second cap, I tried my best to dissuade him from his generosity, but he would not be dissuaded. I took the second capful and with great regret swallowed it, also. It was almost too much for me and I had to break off our meeting. I rushed down the trail drinking and gargling an entire liter of water in an attempt to rid my mouth of the oily taste and douse the flames in my stomach.

Campesinos can be annoying in their insistence on your selling or giving them something. They, children especially, will often ask for candy. *Dame dulce* means "give me candy." It is in just these situations where it is you who has a negative impact upon them. In such a simple exchange, a clash of cultural values takes place, often with serious and detrimental effects on the traditional culture of the campesinos. You should realize that the request stems from the presence of foreigners in their land. Although you have so much in comparison to them, and the simple giving of a small gift seems to do little harm, do consider your actions.

Andean society during the time of the Incas, and even earlier, worked on a system of reciprocity. Services and goods were exchanged to be repaid by other services and goods at a later date. This system still exists in many aspects of the campesino's life. An example of this is the custom whereby one man's fields are planted by the entire community, then he and the rest of the community move on to work another man's fields.

When you give candy or money as charity in the countryside, you are breaking down an age-old custom by giving something for nothing. An old man once asked me for a sip of a cola I was drinking. He wouldn't have asked me if I had been Peruvian, so I refused. Without further supplication or protest,

Campesinos take part in a chaqui taccla, *a communal tilling.*

he simply walked away, his unwarranted request having failed. (The professional beggars of Cuzco and small towns are an exception, but only because they are an integral part of modern society.)

There are situations, however, where you can and should give something in return for a favor or kindness done. I have often been given food or coca leaves by campesinos while hiking, and in return I try to give them something simple and useful. Postcards, tops, sewing needles, medicine, and small mirrors all make appreciated and useful gifts. Out in the country, money should never be given. In a culture that works on reciprocity and barter, the foreign influence of money has deleterious effects.

Perhaps the most important thing to share with campesinos is a bit of yourself, for to thoughtlessly hand out gifts only highlights the differences between your wealth and their poverty. You become the rich gringo, nothing more. Strive for equality and friendship in your brief encounters with these people, avoiding a benefactor-beneficiary relationship.

Animals. The domestic animals the hiker meets along the trail can be anything from a nagging irritation to a potential health threat. Dogs are the most vocal and visibly menacing of these animals. Campesinos often live with several dogs, all of them eager to charge and bark at strangers. To ensure that the canines' actions do not become anything worse than a bark, you should arm yourself with a nearby rock. Merely throwing the rock in the direction of your attacker will achieve a respectful distance between you and him. If there are no suitable rocks close at hand, just fake that you do have a stone, and similar results can be attained. Dogs in the country rarely bite, but do not assume that they won't bite.

When you meet horses or cows along the trail, it is wise to give them a wide berth. A kick from a cow or horse could put a sudden end to a hike and carry with it dangerous medical repercussions for the recipient. A cow's horns are also two points best avoided.

If you meet up with a pack train of llamas coming your way, you need to give these timid, skittish animals an especially wide passage. They are uncomfortable with strangers and tend to stop and stare. Moreover, despite the llama's elegant demeanor, it can reputedly spit like a longshoreman.

Ruins. The Inca and pre-Inca ruins in the Cuzco area have withstood the batterings of weather and encroachment of vegetation for hundreds of years. They will stand for hundreds more if you treat these ancient structures with the care and respect they deserve. Ruins should not be climbed on or over. A heavy hiking boot or even tennis shoe can inflict more damage to brittle stone and adobe walls than years of rain and wind. Unlike Machu Picchu, there is no watchman at remote ruins to blow a whistle when a person starts to climb over walls. So blow your own whistle at yourself and others when you begin to investigate ruins with thoughtless enthusiasm.

You can camp near ruins, but you should not camp within their walls. Above all, fires should not be built against walls.

Besides leaving an ugly black stain, fire weakens the stone through heating and cooling. The above should go without saying, but I've even seen a finely carved stone with an ancient door-latch loop cracked and blackened due to an individual's selfish indifference after being employed as a fire windbreak.

Garbage. I have left discussing this till last, but by no means is trash the least important consideration when in the country. Take it with you. If you can carry it in, you certainly can carry it out. As a rule, leave an area in the same condition as you entered it, or better yet, even cleaner. There are areas along the Inca Trail that look more like the city dump than a wilderness trail. Don't make the problem worse or spread it to other areas.

Body wastes should be buried. Fecal matter carries your foreign germs, which can be transmitted with serious health consequences to local people who live in areas without medical facilities. Burning your toilet paper will also minimize your effect on an area.

Traditions & Beliefs

When the Spanish arrived in Peru, they entered a realm like no other in the world. A great civilization had arisen in the world's most densely populated mountainous region, and, as all great civilizations have done, the Incas had built beautiful temples to their gods, impressive palaces for their rulers, intricate roads for conquests and control, and well-planned cities for their people. All these trappings of civilization fell into disrepair and ruin after the Incas, driven from power, were slowly killed off. Today, mute ruins of a destroyed civilization greet those who visit Peru, but a great civilization is more than the sum of its roads, temples, and palaces. A culture runs deeper than the inanimate structures it builds, for monuments are merely physical expressions of the profound beliefs and traditions held by people.

The Incas were great administrators, hence they institutionalized and codified many of the Andean peoples' strongly held beliefs and customs. They developed a calendar of ceremonies and observances that divided the year into a series of events and that marked plantings, harvestings, and feast days. Much of the raw material for these holidays and agricultural cycles came from beliefs and traditions, the origins of which stretch back beyond the brief rule of the Incas into a dark, unrecorded time.

Although more than four hundred and fifty years have passed since the conquest of the Incas, many of the beliefs and customs of the pre-hispanic world remain. It is true that each town has its Catholic church and that the Quechuas have in part adopted the dress and the devices of Western culture, but more important are the campesinos' beliefs in earth spirits and shadowy ancestral forces as well as the observances surrounding them, all of which still govern their lives.

Pachamama. The belief in Pachamama, the earth-mother, lives on today. Pachamama provides all the necessities of life, from food to the materials needed to build a house. It is from her that all things come and, in the end, to whom they return. The past resides with her, the present is acted out upon her, and the future will be born from her. She controls life while also harboring the dead and their spirits.

Just as the seasons come and go, Pachamama also undergoes a cyclic change. Most of the year, she passively receives the labors of the campesinos, willingly germinating and generating life. Man may cultivate her soil, for she feels no pain and requires nothing in return. On certain days, however, Pachamama comes alive. In these times, the soil cannot be worked; instead, it is a time to bring the earth-mother offerings. Pachamama can be sad or happy, she can speak and cry, and she can reward or punish as she feels proper. She also reveals the future through such signs in the countryside as the level of a stream, the ground beneath a rock, or the position of the moon, all of which indicate coming events.

Pachamama dies every year during Easter week. For seven days she has no control over the evil spirits that inhabit the land and sky, and the countryside becomes a place of danger. The people who live there must take care.

For the campesino, Pachamama lives not as a legend or folktale, but as a very real being. She is the earth and force around which all life must be ordered. Offerings are presented to her, and days set aside to worship her.

Apus. Pachamama resides in all places, but apus are earth spirits that inhabit particular locations. Any natural formation, such as a stream, a lake, or a hill, can be an apu's home. Apus live a hierarchical existence in their relationships with each other and with mankind, their powers in proportion to their geographical size and proximity to humans. Local apus in the hills and streams near a village provide daily protection for the people's crops and animals. Apus that inhabit small peaks control the fertility of fields because the crops are nourished by lake waters nestled at the base of these peaks.

The greatest apus, though, are those that live at the tops of mountain peaks. The large peaks, such as Nv. Ausangate, control animal fertility. They also select the village shamans, the people who have powers to make traditional offerings and cure the sick. It is believed that mountain apus own the riches hidden within their peaks, so offerings are still made today to the mountain apu when a mine is opened, or a road built, along its slope.

Apus can resemble human beings both in appearance and actions. The wild animals of the highlands serve the apu as his domestic creatures. Pumas are his cats, the fox his dog, the vicuna his llama, and the condor both his chicken and sacred messenger. Apus often serve in the legends of the campesinos as models for a virtuous life.

Apus dwell in the mountain landscape of the Andes.

Despite their human characteristics, apus remain all-powerful gods. Ambivalent beings, apus can be beneficent by performing miracles, or malevolent by punishing the disrespectful. Because of their immense powers, apus are greatly feared and respected. Even today people in Cuzco assemble to call upon apus to cure ailments and solve life's problems.

Other Beings. The Andean world is also inhabited by a variety of other beings, all with their own particular histories and powers. Gods that control the weather reside in the high mountains with the apus. Yearly rituals in homage to these gods of rain, hail, and snow are performed to bring about favorable conditions for the growing of crops.

The *antepasados* were the first beings to inhabit the world. Very large and powerful, these beings dwelled in the darkness prior to the sun's creation. When the sun was created — as punishment for transgressions against the gods — the antepasados scattered. Some fled to the darkness of the jungle, others turned to stone to form *huacas* (sacred objects), and others shriveled and sank into the earth to hide in dark places. The rest of the antepasados became evil spirits, called *soq' a-machu, soq' a-paya,* and *soq' a-pujiu,* who are responsible for illness, death, and deformed babies. Other supernatural beings give fertility to animals, play practical jokes on humans, or walk the earth in condemnation for their incestuous relationships.

The mountainous world of the Andes is not just an inanimate place of rocky peaks and fertile valleys. Instead, the Andes are the cradle of a culture that has transformed the mountain winds into passing spirits, rocks into sacred ancestors, and the earth itself into the essential force of life. The magic of the Andes lies not only in the beauty of its landscape but in the Quechua people who dwell there and carry on age-old customs and traditions.

Day-Walks

1

Plaza de Armas to the Ruins of Sacsayhuaman, Qenco, Puca Pucara, & Tambomachy

ELEVATION GAIN: 355 m	LENGTH: 1 day
ELEVATION LOSS: 355 m	DISTANCE: 20 km

The ruins lying just outside of Cuzco have become a sightseeing institution, a must when visiting the city. Yet instead of riding from one ruin to the next in a tour bus, you can walk through the rugged countryside to the sites. Set aside a full day for hiking to and visiting the four ruins along this route. Also, avoid paying the expensive entrance fees by buying a single ticket that allows you admittance into all of the historical sites in the Cuzco region. The ticket is good for ten days, costs US $10 (US $5 for students), and can be bought at the tourist office in the plaza, or at the entrance to Sacsayhuaman. Otherwise, you will be charged separately for each site, as much as US $5 just to see Sacsayhuaman.

The Walk

Begin your walk at the *Plaza de Armas.* Facing the cathedral, you will want to take *Calle Suecia,* which leads uphill at the left-hand corner of the plaza. Follow this street till you reach the road below the church of San Cristobal. From the church walk uphill along the road to the entrance gate below Sacsayhuaman.

Considered by many people to be one of the wonders of the world, the fortress of *Sacsayhuaman* is awe-inspiring in the grandness of its megalithic construction. Built not only as a fortress but as a ceremonial center as well, construction began under the reign of Inca Pachacuti and lasted some sixty years. The three-tiered zigzag walls stretch for 380 meters along the hill's natural incline. Their zigzag design forced attackers to expose their flank to the enemy no matter from what angle they charged the wall. The structure's massive stones were most likely dragged to the site by trains of llamas and men, all pulling together. The largest stone, which forms the apex of two walls, has a height of 8.5 meters and weighs around 110 tons.

In 1933, to mark the 400th anniversary of the Conquest, the hilltop above Sacsayhuaman was excavated, revealing the foundations of Inca buildings and towers. The most impressive find was the circular *Muyuc Marca* tower and its water channels. Unfortunately, these structures did not survive the Conquest due to the pilfering of cut stone, which was used in the construction of the colonial city below.

Rodadero Hill stands across the parade ground, opposite the imposing walls. The Inca's Throne, speculated to be the place from which the Inca watched festivities and rites, is located here. On Rodadero's other side are the smooth natural rock formations that present-day Cuzco families bring their children to play on and slide down. Just beyond the slides are a recently excavated amphitheater and a maze of tunnels winding through carved rocks.

The only battle that Sacsayhuaman saw was in May of 1536. The rebel Manco Inca set fire to Cuzco before retreating to the fortress, which was soon under attack by the conquistadores. Although the Incas lost, Francisco Pizarro's half-brother, Juan, died on the battlefield. The name Sacsayhua-man means Replete Falcon in Quechua, and is in reference to the many carrion-eating birds that gorged themselves here after the defeat of the Incas in their siege of Cuzco.

From Sacsayhuaman, head to the ruin of *Qenco,* several kilometers to the east, by way of the road behind the statue of Jesus. Qenco is a classic example of a *huaca,* a natural rock shrine believed to be sacred. The amphitheater, built beside the outcrop, centers around a large stone pinnacle, which is conjectured to be anything from a giant sundial to a seated puma.

Atop the rock outcrop are numerous carvings. Perhaps the most enigmatic carvings are two short stone cylinders. Victor Angles Vargas, a noted archaeologist, believes the cylinders were used for astronomical observations but does not explain how.

A zigzag channel thought to have been used in divination ceremonies runs close to the edge of the outcrop. Most likely, *chicha* was poured into this channel. Chicha, a concoction brewed from sprouted corn, *jora,* and tasting not unlike the juice from the canned stuff, is still popular among campesinos today. A *chicheria,* a shop that sells chicha, advertises by fly-ing a small red or white flag from a pole, the flag often being a plastic bag or bouquet of geraniums.

Leave Qenco by way of the road heading away from Cuzco. The ruins of *Puca Pucara* are some six kilometers farther down this road, so follow it or walk overland along its left side. Puca Pucara, once a residence for the Inca, is a fine example of how the Incas utilized existing rock outcrops in their structures.

Just beyond the ruins of Puca Pucara is the entrance of *Tambomachay,* known as the *Baño del Inca* — the Inca's bath. The triple waterfall no doubt served in some ritual func-tion, and the site, with its terraces and large niches, seems well-designed for such a purpose.

Return to Cuzco by the same route, or if you are tired you can catch a van or small truck from the roadside.

Caution: In recent years, a number of assaults and robberies have been reported near the sites previously described. The narrow quebradas leading back down into Cuzco are particularly notorious for ambushes and should be avoided. When walking between ruin sites, travel in groups of three or more for safety.

2

Tambomachay to Pisac

ELEVATION GAIN: 400 m   LENGTH: 6 hours
ELEVATION LOSS: 1190 m   DISTANCE: 25 km

A hike from the ruins of Tambomachay to Pisac introduces the traveler to Cuzco's countryside, with its steep hills, small communities, and ancient paths. The trail passes over the mountain ridge between Cuzco and the Sacred Valley before dropping steeply into the valley and on toward the Inca town-site of Pisac.

Time has erased most of an Inca road that once ran between these two sites, but some fragments paralleling the modern roadway can still be seen. The route described here does not follow the Inca road. Instead, it reaches Pisac in a less direct, but more scenic, manner. The trail deserves an early-morning start to ensure that you have plenty of time for walking. Hikers should be prepared with sturdy hiking boots and strong knees for the steep descent into the Sacred Valley. This day walk requires some stamina and hiking ability; therefore, it is not for newcomers to the high country.

How to Get There

Although you can hike to the ruins of Tambomachay from Cuzco, this will add an extra two hours to the walk. Instead, catch a ride in a bus leaving from Av. Tacna and get off ten kilometers from Cuzco at the entrance to the ruins of Tambo-machay. You can also negotiate with a taxi driver in the Plaza de Armas to take you to the trailhead at the ruins.

The Walk

The trail begins a hundred meters farther down the road from the entrance. Start by climbing up the trail, walking through a eucalyptus grove and past a small group of houses. The path then cuts sharply to the right and continues up along the slope. After passing over the ridge and leaving the view of Cuzco behind, the trail forks. Take the trail that leads off to the right, and continue along the slope before descending to the aqueduct just before the village of *Qorimarca.* Walk through the village and onto a broad plain by way of the dirt road.

In the line of mountains on the left, you should see a gap. This is your route. Although not the most direct route to Pisac, it does avoid the paved road. Cross the stream on your left at the footbridge, and continue past a schoolhouse, through the village, and around the hill to the right. Keep heading in the direction of the gap. A stream runs down the hillside. Ascend along its right bank in the direction of the gap before cutting across open fields to the crest.

When you have reached the top, do not descend to the small valley below, but follow the worn, level path leading to the left. At the break in the ridge, three peaks come into view. The mountains of *Pitusiray* and *Siwasiray* stand on the right, and *Nv. Chicon* rises on the left. The trail then descends to the village of *Patabamba.*

In Patabamba, walk through the village by way of a wide lane that turns to the right and brings the *Sacred Valley* into view. Below, the *rio Vilcanota* flows straight through the valley by way of a 3,300-meter-long canal. The Incas built the canal,

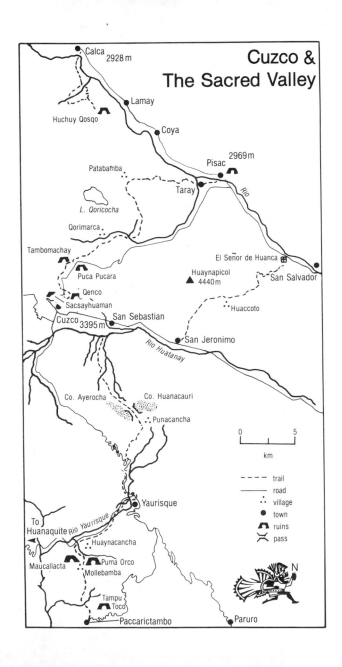

Cuzco &
The Sacred Valley

Calca 2928 m

Lamay

Huchuy Qosqo

Coya

Patabamba

Pisac 2969 m

Taray

Río

L. Qoricocha

Qorimarca

Tambomachay

El Señor de Huanca

Puca Pucara

Huaynapicol ▲ 4440 m

San Salvador

Qenco

Sacsayhuaman

Cuzco 3395 m

San Sebastian

Huaccoto

Río Huatanay

San Jeronimo

Co. Ayerocha

Co. Huanacauri

Punacancha

0   5

km

Yaurisque

To
Huanaquite Río Yaurisque

trail
road
village
town
ruins
pass

Huaynacancha

Puma Orco

Maucallacta

Mollebamba

Tampu
Toco

N

Paccarictambo

Paruro

straightening the river to wrest control of land from its mean-dering waters.

From Patabamba, you begin a bone-and-nerve-jarring descent into the Sacred Valley. Fine sand from the soft white rock of the mountainside covers the trail and makes it quite slick. The day I hiked down this path I was wearing a pair of old tennis shoes with little traction, and I had to practically crab-crawl down the path.

Once the trail levels out, continue up the valley toward *Pisac,* passing through the small town of Taray. Vans and trucks leave from Pisac, heading both down the valley and back to Cuzco.

3

San Jeronimo to the Sanctuary of El Señor de Huanca

ELEVATION GAIN: 990 m
ELEVATION LOSS: 1050 m

LENGTH: 5-6 hours
DISTANCE: 15 km

A modest red-roofed church stands in the upper Sacred Valley above Pisac. It is unexceptional in all aspects except its size, which is way out of proportion to the small town and its few inhabitants nearby. The priests of the Sanctuary of El Señor de Huanca minister to far more people than live in the town, for pilgrims come here from Cuzco and even farther to attend mass. The sanctuary has been a popular pilgrimage destination for hundreds of years.

It started in 1674 when Jesus Christ was reported to have appeared over a rock before the Indian miner Diego Quispe. Shortly thereafter, the rock was painted in commemoration of the miracle. Then, on September 14, 1713, there was another apparition, this time before a wealthy landowner. A sanctuary was built over the stone, and now an annual pilgrimage to the site takes place every September 14th.

Beginning in San Jeronimo, a town just outside of Cuzco, the pilgrimage trail leads out of the valley below Cuzco, over a mountain ridge, and down into the Sacred Valley to the sanctuary. The trail, though well-worn, is steep, rugged, and long.

Hikers should be accustomed to the Andes before attempting the walk.

How to Get There
Buses run to San Jeronimo but are slow, crowded, and frequented by pickpockets, so take a taxi to the main plaza of San Jeronimo for around US $1.

The Walk
You start the hike by walking one block in the direction of Cuzco along the street at the top left-hand corner of the plaza. Then turn right and begin your ascent of the valley side. At first, the trail follows along a stony road through groves of eucalyptus. After rounding a bend, the trail departs from the road. It cuts up through the mountainside but still roughly follows the road, occasionally returning to the dirt track before once again cutting up the slope and bypassing the switchbacks.

You will soon be above the groves of trees, where you will have an unobstructed view of the Cuzco valley. Cuzco itself sits to the west at the valley's end. Cuzco, meaning Navel in Quechua, served as the capital and center of the Inca's vast empire; hence, the city was literally the "navel" of their known world.

Tahuantinsuyu, as the Incas called their empire, means "land of the four quarters." Imaginary lines dividing their world into the four parts of *Chinchaysuyu, Antisuyu, Collasuyu,* and *Cuntisuyu* radiated from Cuzco. Chinchaysuyu, including present-day Ecuador and northern and central Peru, was the northwest quarter. Antisuyu, enclosing the Sacred Valley and the Andes' eastern foothills and forests, was the northeast quarter. Collasuyu, the largest of the four quarters, spread to the southeast and contained the highlands of the Aymara Indians, Lake Titicaca, most of Bolivia, the northwest highlands of Argentina, and northern Chile. The southwest quarter of Cuntisuyu was made up of today's southern Peru.

If you look toward Cuzco, you will see the mountain crag of *Señal Huaynapicol* jutting from the ridge. The trail continues alongside the road until finally crossing a crest in the ridge. On the other side of the ridge, you will see the village of *Huaccoto* on the right. Cross down through the fields and pastures and continue through the village. Just above it, cross to a small stream's opposite bank and climb steeply to the right before reaching a pasture. You can see the rocky crags of *Cerro Pachatusan* in the distance. Make for the pass to the left of the peaks by using the high ground of the hill on the left, thus avoiding the mushy ground of the pasture.

You will find a number of small stone "houses" at the pass (4250 meters). Pilgrims to the sanctuary build these *illas,* or *inqaychus,* to ensure good luck and prosperity for their household in the coming year. Descend from the pass a short way before coming to the ruins of a house. Just beyond the ruins you will find a rock outcrop that provides a sweeping view of the upper *Sacred Valley,* and if you are not careful, a quick plunge to its floor below. Down to the left, an Inca ruin can be seen perched atop a cliff. Most likely, the ruin once served as a watchstation for guarding the valley's upper end.

Near the bottom of the valley on the right, you can see the red roof of the sanctuary. This is your goal, so descend carefully along the steep slope. After leveling out, the trail continues up the valley to the sanctuary, passing fields and small houses.

At the back of the sanctuary, there is a fine little park with benches and trees, perfect for picnicking. Also here are a number of baths where the faithful cleanse themselves in the frigid waters. From the park, look to the mountains you have just descended and see the mines Diego Quispe worked during the seventeenth century.

In the dimly lit sanctuary, the painting of *El Señor de Huanca* is encased in the massive altar. It doesn't look much like a rock, so unbelievers may enter the building from the back, where a portion of the sacred stone is exposed. Legend has it that when the painting fades from view, the world will come to an end. Given the darkened and obscure condition of the image, not much time is left.

The stone of El Señor de Huanca is not an uncommon shrine; other such stones in the region are worshipped. In reality, these rocks are christianized *huacas,* sacred objects. Long before the Inca empire spread throughout the Andes, the Indian worshipped certain stones, believing them to be sacred and powerful. Some peoples of the Andes believe that particular stones are the remains of the world's first race. The world's original inhabitants somehow angered a god, and thus were turned to stone. Worshipped today as ancestors, these stones are scattered across Peru and Bolivia.

To return to Cuzco, catch a ride at the sanctuary or head to the town of *San Salvador* a little farther up the valley. Transportation from San Salvador is irregular, so be there by mid-afternoon. The trip back to Cuzco by way of Pisac takes an hour and a half to two hours.

4

Chinchero to the Sacred Valley
by Inca Road

ELEVATION GAIN: —
ELEVATION LOSS: 900 m

LENGTH: 3-4 hours
DISTANCE: 8 km

The walk from Chinchero down into the Sacred Valley is a perfect way to spend a day outside Cuzco. With an early start, you can visit the village of Chinchero, which rests atop an Inca townsite, walk from there along a steep Inca road to the rio Urubamba below, and still return to Cuzco by nightfall. If you choose to visit Chinchero on a Sunday, when the local market is held, you can buy artifacts and food as well as visit the ruins.

How to Get There

Vans to Chinchero leave daily from Av. Arcopata, an extension of Av. Montero off Saphi. The 30-kilometer drive takes between thirty minutes and an hour. Vans stop at a gatehouse in Chinchero, where tourists are required to show tickets or purchase one for US $2.

The Walk

From the Inca ruins of Chinchero, you can look across the low trough and see a trail on the opposite hill cutting up to the

Crowds gather to shop at the Sunday market in Chinchero.

right. This is the trail to the Sacred Valley. Cross over the trough, and follow the trail up the slope before turning the bend and beginning the descent. The trail stays to the left side of the *quebrada Urquillos* and descends steeply. There are no turnoffs until you reach a small town at the bottom. From here, continue along the road leading down the valley to the town of *Huayllabamba* several kilometers away. At Huayllabamba, a bridge crosses the river to the main road. Return to Cuzco in a small truck or van: by going up the valley you can return to Cuzco by way of Calca and Pisac, and by going down the valley you can return by way of Urubamba and the road that leads back through Chinchero.

The trail from Chinchero to the Sacred Valley is a fine example of Inca roads, which played a key role in uniting and maintaining their empire. Cut stones were planted at angles in the trail to provide footing and to prevent erosion of the path. Campesinos still use the road today to lead laden burros up and down the valley side.

About halfway down, you will come to the ruins of a *tambo,* an Inca posthouse. Tambos dotted the Inca road system at an average of one every five kilometers, and served as rest stops and exchange points for *chaskis,* Inca messengers. The chaski was a member of a select group of messengers formed to carry the Inca's commands and other information to all corners of Tahuantinsuyu. To aid him in transmitting messages, the chaski carried a *quipu,* a knotted and multicolored set of strings that worked on the decimal system. The quipu served as a communication aid only when it was combined with the chaski's memorized information. Otherwise, it was useless. The system of chaskis was so well organized and maintained that the Inca could have fresh fish brought from the sea and served at his table in less than twenty-four hours. A message sent from Cuzco to Quito, some 2000 kilometers (1250 miles) apart, took only three days to arrive.

In Chinchero, you may decide to return directly to Cuzco by way of a different Inca road, one that served as a communication link with Machu Picchu. It runs northwest from the village, connects with the Inca Trail, and terminates at the Lost City of the Incas. The road can be found leading out of Chinchero next to the archway that separates the upper and lower plazas. This route, which runs southeast along a line of mountains for 22 kilometers before reaching Cuzco, takes about five hours to walk.

5

Calca to the Ruins of Huchuy Qosqo

ELEVATION GAIN: 722 m   LENGTH: 4-5 hours
ELEVATION LOSS: 722 m   DISTANCE: 15 km

A couple of hours' walk from the provincial town of Calca in the Sacred Valley leads you to the seldom-visited ruins of Huchuy Qosqo. Spread across a shelf in the mountainside, Huchuy Qosqo commands a spectacular view of the valley surrounding Calca and the mountains of the Cordillera Urubamba towering high behind it. Of all the walks presented, this one is my favorite. The trail follows a rushing stream up a narrow quebrada before cutting over to the mountain slope high above the Sacred Valley and the ruins. The trail is wide and not very steep, providing an intermediate hike.

How to Get There

The quickest and most convenient way to arrive at Calca is to take a minibus from Av. Tacna. See the transportation section on the Sacred Valley in the introduction.

The Walk

The walk to Huchuy Qosqo begins in the central plaza of Calca and takes from two to three hours. Walk down to the *rio*

Vilcanota by way of *Calle Garcilaso.* Cross the river at the suspension bridge, turn left, and walk upriver along the Vilcanota for several kilometers. As you near the quebrada to the right, take any of the trails heading toward it. The trails will join and then curve through the quebrada along a cascading stream. At a rushing channel in the stream, the trail crosses to the right bank. A little farther on, it crosses back to the left bank to run beside a wall. Crossing over again to the right bank, you will come to a relatively flat, overgrown field, the quebrada curving sharply to the left ahead. Do not continue up the quebrada, but follow a small trail to the brush-covered banks of the stream, which you should then cross once more.

The trail widens and climbs the steep slope of the quebrada, heading back in the direction of the Sacred Valley. At the ruins of a house, you will reach a high point that overlooks the valley. To your left, you can see the peaks of *Pitusiray* and *Siwasiray* above Calca, and, farther down the valley, *Nv. Chicon.* To your right, the ruins of Huchuy Qosqo stand along the valley's side.

Legend has it that the peaks of Pitusiray and Siwasiray were once members of the Inca nobility. They were lovers, but their fathers forbade them to see each other. They disobeyed and were turned to stone in punishment. To this day, the spirits of the tragic lovers are believed to dwell inside the mountains as apus.

When I first arrived at *Huchuy Qosqo,* I was surprised to see just how extensive the ruins are. Mystery surrounds their origins, but John Hemming, in his *Monuments of the Incas,* writes that the ruins might be the *Caquia Xaquixahuana* mentioned by Pedro de Cieza de Leon and other chroniclers after the Conquest. The construction of Huchuy Qosqo, which means Small Cuzco in Quechua, was carried out as tribute by the tribe inhabiting Calca after it was subjugated by the eighth Inca ruler, Viracocha. It was customary for each lord Inca to

The ruins of Huchuy Qosqo overlook the Sacred Valley.

have a palace built in the country as a retreat and place of relaxation.

These ruins, which spread over a kilometer long, must have once made a fine retreat, with their beautiful view of the valley and with Sacsayhuaman only 20 kilometers away by Inca road. As you enter into the ruins, you can see a small reservoir that is choked with weeds but still functions. The gateway providing access to Huchuy Qosqo for the road from Cuzco stands slightly above the ruins in the direction of the upper valley. The main buildings are grouped around a walled-in, sunken area that may have served as a swimming pool, though no water channel is apparent. Located in a far upper corner of the complex, a stone enclosed by high walls and large niches is reminiscent of the pinnacle at Qenco, but its sacred function has been lost to time.

At the main plaza, a long building with six doorways stands above the terrace wall. This is a *kallanka,* a large building that once had a peaked roof covering it. These structures were constructed around the main plazas in the principal towns of the empire to house soldiers, laborers, and other transient people. It was from buildings like this one that Pizarro and his men made their desperate charge on the Inca Atahualpa at Cajamarca, capturing him and massacring thousands of his Indian troops.

To return to Calca, you can either follow the same route back, or at the ruins of the house take the switchback trail. Although the switchback provides a faster and more direct route to the valley, it is quite steep and dangerous.

6

Ollantaytambo to the Ruins of Pumamarca

ELEVATION GAIN: 750 m
ELEVATION LOSS: 750 m

LENGTH: 4 hours
DISTANCE: 8 km

Ollantaytambo is the site of a magnificent Inca fortress believed to have been begun under the rule of Pachacuti but never finished because of the Spanish invasion. Standing guard at the conjunction of the quebrada Patacancha and the rio Urubamba in the Sacred Valley, the ruins serve as a trailhead to Pumamarca. An easy walk above Ollantaytambo along the Patacancha brings the hiker to the ruins of Pumamarca. The hike is not strenuous and is an enjoyable way to spend a morning or afternoon exercising and adjusting to the altitude.

How to Get There

From Cuzco, you can reach Ollantaytambo either by a train from the San Pedro terminal or by a van from Av. Huascar 128. Vans sometimes go directly to Ollantaytambo, but more likely than not you'll need to take a truck from Urubamba to the town.

The Walk

You can start the walk either from the ruins of Ollantay-tambo, or at the road that leads from between the two plazas of the town up the *Patacancha*. From the ruins, walk up the valley until the trail finally converges with the road and stream. The road from between the two plazas passes by houses and stays on the right bank of the stream before crossing a bridge and joining with the trail from the ruins.

Follow the trail along the stream's left bank past a row of houses. At the end of these houses stands a two-story, white-washed building with a corrugated roof. The trail leads behind this house and follows along a mountain spur. At the entrance gate to the terraces, the trail switches back, running up along the spur. Continue along this easily followed path to the ruins of *Pumamarca*. Walking from Ollantaytambo to the ruins takes about two hours.

The trail passes along a mountainside that had been extensively terraced in Incan times. Although some of the terraces have been reconstructed and are in use, most lie in a state of disrepair. Terraces were utilized before the Incas, but it was they who spread them throughout their realm. Used to expand an area under cultivation, terraces also helped to deter erosion along the steep mountainsides.

Terraces had to be carefully planned and constructed. On steep slopes, terraces measured no more than 1.5 meters wide, while near the valley floors they often attained the size of a small farm. As you can see by the terraces around Ollantaytambo, they also conformed to the contours of the mountainsides. In order to build a terrace, its wall was constructed first and at a slight incline to hold the soil. Then, the base was filled with rubble and the top with fertile soil brought from the valley floor. Finally, channels were cut into the stone blocks to allow better drainage.

Terraces were only a small part of the Inca's highly organized agrarian empire. Religious ceremonies and rituals regulating the cultivation of crops were held throughout the year. Also, Inca officials promoted a wider cultivation of corn, while de-emphasizing the planting of potatoes.

Enter Pumamarca from either its uphill or downhill points. The fortress wall has collapsed at these points, allowing easy access to the inner structures. Some people believe that because of its rather crude stonework, Pumamarca may have pre-Inca origins. The ruins were undoubtedly a fortress complex with storage buildings outside a circular main wall that mimics the zigzag contours of Sacsayhuaman's defensive walls. The complex overlooks the conjunction of the streams *Yurajmayu* and *Wanker Chaka*, which join to form the *Patacancha*, and guards the two valleys of these streams.

Return to Ollantaytambo by the same route you arrived at Pumamarca.

A man puts the finishing touches on a new pond.

7

The Salt Ponds of Maras

ELEVATION GAIN: —   LENGTH: 3-4 hours
ELEVATION LOSS: 535 m   DISTANCE: 10 km

In a narrow, steep quebrada cutting through the plateau above the Sacred Valley, the people of Maras have been gathering salt for hundreds of years. A saline stream emerges from the ground to flow down the quebrada through a labyrinth of aqueducts and ponds, encrusting everything in its wake in a brilliant snow of sodium chloride crystals. The *salineras de Maras,* salt ponds of Maras, lie an easy walk down from the plateau. A visit to the salt ponds can be combined with a trip to either Chinchero or Ollantaytambo.

How to Get There
To hike down through the salt ponds, you will need to get to the trailhead, which is located on the road between Urubamba and Chinchero. Trucks and vans travel between Chinchero and Urubamba, but you must first arrive at one of these towns. See the transportation section in the introduction on how to arrive at Urubamba. Vans to Chinchero leave from Av. Arcopata, an extension of Av. Montero off Saphi.

At Urubamba wait near the bridge crossing the river for a truck to Chinchero. In Chinchero trucks heading to Urubamba pass along the main road. No matter what town you are coming from, let the driver know you want off near Tiobamba where a sign marks the turnoff for the road to Maras.

The Walk

Follow the dirt road toward the town of Maras. When the road branches, take the fork to the right, which leads to the quebrada and salt ponds. Some four kilometers from the main road you'll come to storage sheds, where you will be asked to pay a small entrance fee, US $.75, levied by the town government. Continue down the left side of the quebrada, where hundreds of *posas,* ponds, have been constructed. If you leave the main trail and venture onto the network of paths winding through the ponds, be careful not to damage any of the pond walls or aqueducts.

A small chapel overlooking the ponds marks where the saline stream emerges from the ground. Just across from the chapel, on the opposite side of the quebrada, stands an Inca storehouse. The ponds have been worked since, and perhaps prior to, the time of the Incas. The Incas traded the salt for tropical goods with jungle tribes across the Cordillera Urubamba to the north. Today, trucks arrive at the storehouses to purchase the salt, which is then distributed throughout the region.

The oldest ponds are at the top of the quebrada, with newer additions stretching down its length. The ponds are worked from April to October, when the dry season allows for the evaporation of water. Each pond is filled with approximately ten centimeters (four inches) of water, and as the water evaporates, salt crystals are left behind. The salt is then scraped with a board into piles and bagged. A normal-sized pond takes three to four days to dry and produces twenty kilograms of salt, or one hundred fifty kilograms a month. Ponds are owned by families, with each family owning between fifteen and twenty ponds. The town government has a monopoly on the salt, which it buys from the families and then resells to outsiders.

As you leave the ponds at the lower end of the quebrada, you can look across to the right side and see *chullpas,* tombs, which once housed the bodies of pre-Columbian Indians. At the juncture of the quebrada and the Sacred Valley, you cross to the right side of the stream and continue past a modern cemetery before reaching a suspension bridge crossing the *rio Urubamba.* Follow the dirt road to Tarabamba, which lies along the main road between Urubamba and Ollantaytambo. At the road you can catch a small truck heading in either direction.

Alternate Route

If you want to visit the salt ponds from the Sacred Valley, you can get off at Tarabamba some 5 kilometers from Urubamba and 14 kilometers from Ollantaytambo. No signs mark the village, so be sure to let the driver know where you want off. The trail begins as a dirt road running down to the river between a wall and line of trees. Follow the trail until you cross the river, and then ascend into the quebrada.

A woman weaves sack cloth in the village of Punacancha.

8

Cuzco to Paccarictambo

ELEVATION GAIN: 650 m   LENGTH: 2 days
ELEVATION LOSS: 870 m   DISTANCE: 35 km

If you are looking for a hike with mountaintop vistas, shining-blue lakes, and narrow highland trails, don't go to Paccarictambo. But if you want a trail that leads back into legend, a hike that contrasts the ancient world with the present-day one, and a feel for the lives of many contemporary Peruvians, walk to Paccarictambo.

The hike to this small town that lies south of Cuzco and near the rio Apurimac takes only two days, requires little equipment or trail experience, and passes several ruins on an Inca road. Although the walk takes more than a day, I have included it in the day-walk section because little equipment is required for the hike. A tent is not necessary, since a simple bed may be found in the towns of Yaurisque and Paccarictambo. A sleeping bag, however, will provide a measure of comfort in these rustic accommodations. One essential piece of equipment that you will want to take along is a good sense of humor to buffer you against the unexpected.

The Trek

To get started, this hike requires just a short trip out to the *aeropuerto*. Take a bus or taxi to the aeropuerto and then walk back to where the road enters it. At the ravine to the road's side, a small footbridge crosses the river, which is now used as a flowing garbage dump. Climb to the railroad tracks on the opposite side. Follow the tracks down the valley beyond the air terminal until you come to a dirt road leading to the right. Follow the road as it rises through fields and pastures toward the hill in the distance.

Once you reach the hill, the trail turns left and runs along its base, heading southeast. As you climb away from Cuzco, the mountains of the *Cordillera Urubamba* appear over the hills opposite the city. The trail remains on the right slope as it ascends to the gap between *Cerro Huanacauri* and *Cerro Ayerocha.* A short distance before the gap you will come upon the ruins of an Incan *tambo* (posthouse). From the gap you walk down to the village of *Punacancha,* four hours from the aeropuerto.

The most important *huaca* of the Incas, *Cerro Huanacauri* has been stripped of any sacred stones or structures that once graced its crest. Part of the Inca's lengthy coronation took place on the hill, as did much of the ceremonial rites of passage for Inca youth. *Capac Raymi,* the yearly initiation of young nobles, centered around Huanacauri. According to Hemming, entire families would fast prior to the pilgrimage of their ornately dressed boys to the hill. Once there, the youth flagellated themselves, danced, and made offerings. Their elders contributed by admonishing them to be brave. Then the event was completed by a footrace to the bottom of the hill.

From Punacancha to *Yaurisque* takes three hours of walking down hills and roads. Start out from Punacancha by following the trail to the right, heading southwest. The last vestiges of Inca road work can be seen as the trail rounds a rocky crag and then winds through a patchwork of fields and pastures. Follow the trail along the right-hand slope. At times, it will disappear in the fields, but you should continue to gradually descend to the valley below. The trail meets the main road one hour above Yaurisque. Follow the road into town.

Yaurisque typifies a Peruvian roadside town. Even though it is only a short distance from Cuzco, the town is nevertheless without electricity. Pigs, cows, and sheep wander freely about the streets. The fact that gringo visitors to town are not only a rarity but quite a novelty as well was testified to by a group of fifteen children who tailed me through the streets when I arrived.

Accommodations and a hot meal can be found by asking around. My room had a bird's-eye view of the animal pen, which served as both my toilet and, because of the water spigot there, washroom. The room itself had a lumpy and torturous bed, along with an ensemble of boards fashioned into a creaky nightstand. Nothing else. I cheated the diabolical bed by smoothing the lumps out with my sleeping bag. The following night, in Paccarictambo, I was not so lucky. An old woman offered me a bed made of filthy sheepskins spread across a dingy mattress. After I accepted these quaint, provincial lodgings, her daughter entered the room, packed up all this unhygienic bedding, and left me with nothing but the naked bed slats.

The next morning, follow the trail from Yaurisque to the village of *Mollebamba*, three hours away. From the plaza, take the road that leads down the valley toward *Hauynacancha*. The road heads southwest past haciendas, pastures, and fields. At the town of Huaynacancha, you cross a concrete bridge. To the left of the bridge, an abandoned road leads up a short side valley. The village of Mollebamba can be seen atop a knoll in the valley. Follow the road along the right slope, saving time by cutting across its switchbacks. The road ends and you must follow the trail along the slope to Mollebamba.

Facing back down the valley from Mollebamba, you can see the ruins of *Maucallacta* on a shelf in the ridge to the left.

Spend some time exploring these ruins, which lie a half hour from the village. A rock outcrop called *Puma Orco* stands on the opposite side of Mollebamba. The name of this carved huaca comes from the puma shaped in the stone. A tunnel can be found at the rock's base and it also has been carved by the Incas.

You continue from Mollebamba to *Paccarictambo,* two and a half hours away. The trail leads out of the village by climbing steeply up the ridge, but it is a wide and easily followed path. The top of the ridge reveals a complex of valleys and hills below. The trail continues to the left, crossing a flat plain. Follow the trail down a quebrada to a lower valley, which the trail does not lead down. Instead, it turns left to once again ascend a hill. Near the hilltop, the trail broadens and finally joins a road a short distance before Paccarictambo. The town is spread out along a hillside, looking out across knife-edged ridges and a deep valley that leads to the mighty rio Apurimac.

When I entered Paccarictambo, I immediately encountered the town mayor, who was quite drunk at the time. His drunkenness had put him in an official state of mind. So, upon seeing me, he asked to see my documents, something every Peruvian must have. Before I could show him identification, he began to lead me down the hill, but then turned and walked a block over, and finally backtracked by leading me up the hill on the next street over. By this roundabout course we at last reached his office.

His office was housed in a thatched-roof, adobe hut, its interior decorated with posters of Juan Velasco — the military ruler of Peru who was deposed of in 1975 — exhorting "Viva la revolucion!" Once again, the mayor demanded to see my Peruvian documents. It took some time before I could convince him that because I was not Peruvian, I had no such documents. I showed him a photocopy of my passport, but still he was not satisfied. Only after a great deal of arguing did he finally accept the reproduction.

Looking at the creased paper, he then commenced to copy my name down. Next, he wrote "Date of Birth," failing to include the actual date. To leave no room for doubt, he also copied the French translation for date of birth. After noting the name of the notary public who had validated the photocopy, he transcribed, with my help, the entire declaration of authenticity. Finally, he made me sign my name beneath all the data he had gathered. But he was not happy in the least bit with my signature. Something was missing. He indicated with wild flailing arms that I had not included a pen flourish beneath my name. Once I did so, I was at long last allowed to leave his office and to even remain in town.

Trucks for Cuzco leave from the lower plaza of the town. Before you leave, you may want to hike several kilometers out of town to the site of *Tampu Toco,* the House of Windows. Tampu Toco is a fixture in one of the legends that explain the birth of the Inca civilization. The most common legend tells that the first Inca, Manco Capac, appeared on the Isla del Sol in Lake Titicaca before setting out to found Cuzco and the empire. The other tale concerns the four Ayar brothers and their four sisters, all of whom emerged from Tampu Toco, a series of openings in the mountainside.

Ayar Auca, Ayar Cache, Ayar Ucho, and Manco Capac were the four brothers. One by one, three of the brothers were either transformed or died until only Manco Capac was left to rule Cuzco. Ayar Cache was so strong he could carve out valleys with stones from his sling. Fearing his strength, the other brothers sent him to Tampu Toco on a ruse to retrieve some belongings they had left there. Once Ayar Cache was inside the mountain, they trapped him there by blocking the doorway with a stone. Ayar Ucho was turned to stone atop

Huanacauri and so became the huaca there. Ayar Auca, upon taking possession of the land at Cuzco, simply vanished at the site of the Qoricancha. Thus, with all his brothers gone but immortalized, Manco Capac began, with the aid of his sisters, the civilization that was to be the most powerful in all the pre-Columbia Americas.

Treks

1

The Inca Trail

ELEVATION GAIN: 2000 m
ELEVATION LOSS: 1800 m

LENGTH: 3-4 days
DISTANCE: 43 km

For the adventurous traveler, a hike along the Inca Trail to Machu Picchu can be the crowning experience of a South American vacation. This remote path takes you through some of the continent's most enchanting scenery, from desertlike sierra to semitropical jungle. Magnificent Inca ruins also punctuate your progress along the trail. When you finally enter Machu Picchu through Intipunku, the Gate of the Sun, it is with a sense of accomplishment and wonder. You have come the way of the Incas, and now gaze down upon their spectacular city.

The popularity of the Inca Trail has skyrocketed in recent years. Some five to six thousand hikers make their way over the ancient trail every year. With this gringo onslaught have come such problems as garbage, robbery, and destruction of the ruins, and only piecemeal efforts to control them have been made. Cleanup crews periodically scour the trail to pick up garbage left by thoughtless hikers. Thieves have been arrested, but no full-time park officials patrol the trail. Four camping areas along the trail have been officially designated, but not equipped. In order to minimize your impact on the trail, you should use these areas as you hike toward Machu Picchu.

How to Get There

Traditionally, the jumping-off point for the Inca Trail is Km 88. To reach Km 88, your options are limited to one: the local train. The 88 in Km 88 refers to the 88th kilometer of the Cuzco-to-Quillabamba train route. At this writing, the local train leaves at 5:30 a.m. and 2:00 p.m., and reaches the trail-head some three hours later. Only the local train, not the tourist train, will stop at Km 88. It is best to buy your ticket in advance.

At Km 88, you will be met by a man in a hard hat with a brief-case in hand. Despite his unlikely dress, he is the official gate-keeper to the Inca Trail and is placed there by the INC, *Instituto Nacional de Cultura.* He will exact from you entrance fees to both the trail and Machu Picchu. Currently, tickets run about US $15 for foreigners.

The Trek

Once you have paid the gatekeeper, cross the suspension bridge over the rio Urubamba, then follow the trail upriver, gradually ascending through a grove of eucalyptus trees. You will come to the ruins of *Llactapata,* where you turn right and walk past the terraces of the complex. Located near the ruins is the first designated campsite along the Inca Trail.

The extensive ruins of *Llactapata* are worth exploring. Archaeologists have estimated that under the rule of the Incas the area produced three times the food it needed to sustain its inhabitants. Such an excess of production was not unusual in the Inca empire. As a general rule, the Incas required their subjects to give a third of their annual production to the state, and another third to the religious cult of the sun. The final third remained for the inhabitants. These great stores of food for the state and the religious cult were then used to support the administration of the empire, feed the massive work forces required for state projects, supply the Incan armies on their journeys of conquest, and ensure against famine in poor-crop years.

From Llactapata, the trail turns away from the river and continues up the side valley of the *quebrada Cusichaca,* following its rushing waters to the village of *Huayllabamba,* two and a half hours away. At the end of the ruins, cross to the left of the stream and climb a knoll. Continue along this slope, passing fields and numerous houses until shortly before the village, where you again cross the stream by bridge. Walk through the village of Huayllabamba.

From Huayllabamba, the trail turns to the right and leads up the valley of the *quebrada Llullucha.* The pass lies some four and a half hours away from the village. A designated campsite in *Llulluchapampa* lies two-thirds of the way up the trail. Follow the trail up the left slope of the stream. You will come to a small pasture, where the trail forks. Take the right-hand path, which leads through the pasture. You will come to a footbridge that crosses a stream named *Huayruro,* which flows into the Llullucha a short distance below. From the footbridge, turn right and round the spur that separates the two streams. Continue along the left bank of the Llullucha. You will then climb through a lush forest. Breaking from the woods, you will come to the puna of *Llullucha Pampa* and its campsites.

From Llullucha Pampa, the trail continues on the left slope and climbs steadily to the pass. At the *Abra de Huarmihuañusca,* Dead Woman Pass (origin of name unknown), you can look out from your 4198-meter perch to survey the mountainscapes on either side of the pass. The circular ruins of Runkuracay stand in the distance on the left-hand slope. Closer to Huarmihuañusca, on the same slope, a small trail winds up the steep side and crosses the ridge. This is the trail to the ruins of Palcay and is also an alternative route to the ruins of Sayajmarca.

The most commonly used route of the Inca Trail descends down into the valley of the *rio Pacaymayu,* where the trail's third official campsite can be found an hour and a half from Huarmihuañusca. The trail is well-worn and easily followed, yet should not be followed past the camp area. Faint trails run beside the river but are only to be used by those persons looking to get lost. The trail crosses the Pacaymayu near the campsite, where you can spend the night, and then climbs the left slope to the ruins of *Runkuracay.* From the campsite, the ruins lie an hour away by way of a switchback trail.

Runkuracay is the first ruin of the Inca Trail left undiscovered by the conquistadores. Because most of the ruins along the trail and even Machu Picchu itself were never discovered by the conquerors, the sites have provided archaeologists with an undisturbed physical record of the Incas. Runkuracay's oval structure once functioned as a watch-station overlooking the Pacaymayu valley and, most likely, as a tambo, or rest area, for chaskis and caravans.

From the ruins, the trail leads directly up the slope. Here you can begin to see the remains of a cobbled road, something more elaborate than the dirt path, which contains only fragmentary indications of Inca stonework, that you have been following. Between the ruins and the pass, you come to the stagnant waters of *Yanacocha,* Black Lake. The *Abra de Runkuracay* lies at 3398 meters, less than an hour away from the ruins it takes its name from. Once you attain this pass, you may breathe a little easier, for the trail's gradients become much more gentle and head mostly downward in direction.

From the pass, continue down the left slope of the valley to the ruins of *Sayajmarca,* an hour and a half away. As you make your way along the Inca Trail to its three major ruins,

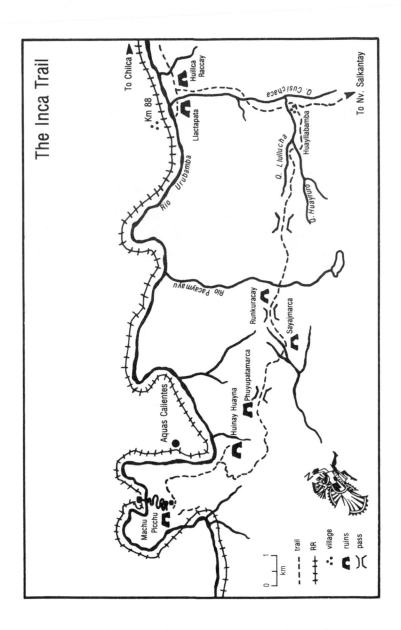

The Inca Trail

To Chilca
Km 88
Huilca Raccay
Llactapata
Q. Cusichaca
Huayllabamba
To Nv. Salkantay
Q. Llullucha
Q. Huayruro
Rio Urubamba
Rio Pacaymayu
Runkuracay
Sayajmarca
Phuyupatamarca
Huinay Huayna
Aquas Calientes
Machu Picchu

trail
RR
village
ruins
pass

0   1
km

The gracefully curved walls of Sayajmarca look out over a deep valley.

you will notice that the road's stonework becomes progressively more sophisticated and stunning in design. Rounding a bend in the valley, you come into view of Sayajmarca perched atop a mountain spur. Continue down the trail to a steep set of stairs and climb them to the ruins above.

Perhaps the most spectacular Inca site on the Trail, *Sayajmarca* was discovered by Hiram Bingham in 1915. The famous, often-fanciful explorer named the ruins *Cedrobamba,* meaning Plain of Cedars. This name, however, does not conform to the geography of the region, or to its botany. Neither a plain nor a cedar exists in these valleys. When Paul Fejos visited the site in 1940 with the Wenner Gren Scientific Expedition, he renamed the ruins Sayajmarca, which means Inaccessible Place, an apt description for ruins on a promontory such as this.

Sayajmarca has no terracing around it, but stands
and compact above the valley floor. Within the site th
twenty-one rooms and three ceremonial baths. A four
has been discovered outside the wall near the stairway. A
second entrance to the ruins lies on the opposite side of the
promontory and provides access to the trail that crosses the
ridge before Runkuracay. The cramped quarters of the site,
unique among Inca sites in the region, gives Sayajmarca the
feel of an outpost rather than of a place designed for perma-
nent and comfortable habitation.

To continue along the Inca Trail, descend the steps by
which you entered the ruins. At their base, the trail turns down
toward the ravine below. The woods and brush of this area
harbor a number of voracious insects. The worst of these is
the *pumawacachi,* "bug-that-makes-the-puma-cry." This tiny
black fly upends itself in the process of taking a miniscule-but-
painful bite out of you.

Phuyupatamarca, some two and a half hours from Sayajmarca, is the next site situated along the trail. The trail follows
along the side of the mountain ridge, the cobbled way becom-
ing increasingly fine as it ascends from the ravine. Raised
above the grassy upper pasture by an embankment, the road
measures some two meters across. It then hugs the side of
the ridge, skirting a twenty-meter drop and passing through a
mountainside tunnel. To make the tunnel, the Incas enlarged
the natural crevice in the mountain and incorporated it into
their road.

This short length of road serves as just a small sample of
the technical wizardry the Incas utilized in constructing
15,000 miles of roads throughout their empire. The royal
Andean road alone stretched 5,200 kilometers (3,250 miles),
from the rio Ancasmayo in Colombia to the Tucuman in Chile;
it was a road longer than the Romans' longest, which
stretched from Hadrian's Wall in Scotland to Jerusalem. The

The trail hugs the steep mountainside near Phuyupatamarca.

main coastal road ran for 4,030 kilometers (2,520 miles) along the desert. Unsurfaced, it measured a uniform width of 5 meters. Both of these major highways were interconnected by roads running from sea level up to the highest valleys and passes of the mountains. The highest road runs over a pass of Nv. Salkantay at 5000 meters. The highland roads varied in width, measuring from 1.5 meters in difficult terrain to 6 meters in the broad valleys. Suspension bridges of twined hemp were built to allow transportation across the raging rivers of the Andes. A young Thornton Wilder immortalized one such bridge that crossed the Apurimac in his book *The Bridge of San Luis Rey.*

The third and final pass of the Inca Trail lies just before the ruins of Phuyupatamarca. The INC, which is currently restoring the trail and its ruins, has moved campsites from out of the ruins of Phuyupatamarca to the ridges 100 meters above it.

Although this is beneficial to the preservation of the ruins, you must now walk down to the ruins to obtain water for camp.

A special note to the scenically inspired: A fairweather climb at sunrise or sunset to the peaks above the ruins will reward you with a spectacular view of *Nv. Salkantay* and the surrounding *Cordillera Vilcabamba.*

Hiram Bingham also discovered *Phuyupatamarca.* This time he aptly named the ruins to mean Cloud-Level Town. The 3627-meter elevation places the site right where clouds rising from the jungle region of the rio Urubamba cling to the mountainsides. The site sits on a fifty-degree slope protected on both sides by ridges. The *quebrada Choquesuysuy* flows through the site and furnishes water for its six baths. The INC recently cleaned the stonework, revealing the shining white granite of the structures. When Paul Fejos arrived here in 1940 to begin investigating the Inca Trail ruins, the situation was quite different. Hundreds of years of jungle growth had engulfed the ruins, and intensive labor was required to reveal them. During 1940 and 1941, as many as nine hundred people were employed to clear the sites along the trail. At Phuyupatamarca, a 1.5-meter layer of humus and moss was removed from the upper plaza before reaching its solid-rock surface.

Recent clearing and construction has revealed a new trail leading down hundreds of steps from Phuyupatamarca to the ruins of *Huiñay Huayna,* two and a half hours away. This section, opened in 1984, replaces a section of trail that was not even Incan. Numbering over a thousand, steps beginning in the ruins of Phuyupatamarca do not end at the buildings but continue down the slope. Descending them, you pass a rock alcove that has been divided in two by a low wall with niches. There is yet another tunnel, this one more finely worked than the tunnel before Phuyupatamarca. From some of the trail's ledges overlooking the valley it is possible to see the ruins of

Phuyupatamarca has a near-magical quality about it.

Huiñay Huayna and, lying a short distance away, a tourist hotel. The cobbled path also passes a small group of buildings, probably once a tambo on this ancient route.

The Inca road ends abruptly, the smooth stone trail turning into a sandy track that zigzags its way down past powerlines to the tourist hotel, where there is an area for camping. The ruins of *Huiñay Huayna,* meaning Eternal Youth, stand a short distance from the hotel. Signs at the hotel point the way. Hiram Bingham did not discover these ruins; instead, Huiñay Huayna was not uncovered until Paul Fejos made his explorations of the area in the early forties.

From Huiñay Huayna, only the last leg of the Inca Trail lies between you and Machu Picchu. The trail levels off and heads in a downriver direction high along the ridge above the rio Urubamba. This portion of the trail takes some two to three hours to complete. The ridge is covered with dense vegetation and, far below, the waters of the Urubamba rush along their course

to the Amazon, where they will join in the flow to t
This part of the trail traverses several worn wood
and passes some rather enigmatic stone structure

You will climb a length of stone steps before cor
ruins of a gatehouse. Beyond these are the buildir
punku, the Gate of the Sun. You are now standing at the entrance to Machu Picchu, the lost city of the Incas. Before you
rises the 2743-meter-high sugarloaf of Huayna Picchu, and
below you, spread along the mountain saddle, stands the city
and final destination of the Inca Trail, Machu Picchu.

Walks In and Around Machu Picchu
At Machu Picchu, there are two popular walks that lead you
outside the general area of the ruins. One trail runs southeast
past the cemetery to the *Inca Drawbridge.* In the Incas'
travels to and from the city, this trail provided the only alternative route to the Inca Trail. It narrows until only a buttress supports the path against the sheer cliff face. At midpoint along
the cliff, the buttress contains a gap bridged by long planks,
which the Incas could easily withdraw in case of attack.

The second walk within the ruins leads to the top of Huayna
Picchu. For the physically fit, the climb up the stone steps
takes less than an hour. The peak of Huayna Picchu offers a
spectacular view of the ruins and surrounding valley.

For those people who do not stay at the hotel next to Machu
Picchu but stay at the less expensive accommodations in the
town of Aquas Calientes, you might consider a hike from the
town to Machu Picchu by way of Huiñay Huayna and the final
portion of the Inca Trail. From Aquas Calientes, you walk
upriver to Km 107, where you cross the river at the dam. A trail
then leads up the steep slope to the tourist hotel and ruins.
Continue along the Inca Trail to Machu Picchu. Including time
to view Huiñay Huayna, this route takes six hours to hike.

The Huayanay mountains tower above the village of Quesca.

2

Chilca to Huayllabamba

ELEVATION GAIN: 1870 m   LENGTH: 2-3 days
ELEVATION LOSS: 1860 m   DISTANCE: 30 km

For those hikers who would like to add anywhere from one to three extra days to their Inca Trail trek, the town of Chilca provides a perfect starting point. One route will extend your trek to Machu Picchu by a day. You follow the trail out of Chilca along the left bank of the rio Urubamba, and passing over a level desert landscape for four hours, you arrive at the ruins of Huillca Raccay, which overlook Llactapata. It is only a short, steep descent beyond these ruins to where the path joins the main trail to Machu Picchu.

The other route, which is described below, does not run along the river but instead ascends into the mountains above Chilca. The trail crosses a pass between Nevados Salkantay Este and Huayanay before descending to the stream above Huayllabamba and the Inca Trail. Passing some of the finest mountain scenery of any of the hikes, this short route also runs by Inca ruins, Andean pastures, and small communities. Because you gain and lose nearly as much elevation on this route as you do once you enter the Inca Trail, your trek to Machu Picchu becomes almost twice as long and twice as strenuous as a trek from Km 88.

88

How to Get There

The best way to reach Chilca is to take a local train bound for Quillabamba. Chilca lies some two and a half hours by train outside Cuzco. When you near your destination, be ready to exit quickly from the train, since it will make only a brief stop here.

There is a road from Ollantaytambo to Chilca, but transportation between the two towns is infrequent. It is best to stay with the train.

Andean Goose

The Trek

In Chilca, walk down the lane to the bridge that crosses the Urubamba. Take the trail to the left of the bridge, and follow it toward the broad fields that spread across the entrance to a quebrada. On a spur jutting into the valley, an Inca ruin that may have served as a watch-station for monitoring the movement of people and goods can be seen.

The trail ascends the quebrada, providing a beautiful view of *Nv. Veronica,* at 5750 meters. After passing by the fields, the trail climbs steeply through a heavily vegetated area before reaching a line of trees and level area some one and a half to two hours from Chilca. The trail continues up the narrowing quebrada, switching from side to side and requiring several fordings of the stream. After two hours in this lush ravine, you come to a steep but more open area of the stream. Two more hours of hiking bring you to the village of *Ancascocha.*

At Ancascocha the trail veers right, crossing the unbridged stream and passing the scattered houses of the village. Do not continue up the same valley that you have been walking through since Chilca, but keep right to enter a valley heading southwest. Ancascocha is also the juncture with the trail from Ollantaytambo that runs over the mountains to the east. In the pastures off to the right of the village, you will find two waterfalls cascading from the mountains. Make camp near the waterfalls, or continue a short distance up the valley before stopping for the night.

After breaking camp the next morning, continue up the valley. From the village of Ancascocha to the pass between the peaks of *Salkantay Este* and *Huayanay* takes about two and a half hours to hike. First, you will come to *Laguna Ancascocha,* from which the village derives its name. On the lake's waters, which sit below Nv. Huayanay's towering white face, you might spot the Andean goose *(Cloephage melanoptera),* known in Quechua as a *huayllata.* Found throughout the highlands, the large, white goose has black-tipped wings that merge with a black tail when not in flight. If the sun is out and you are feeling brave enough, you might attempt a dip in the refreshing-yet-frigid waters of the lake. When I took such a plunge, my screams and frenzied splashing unfortunately frightened off all the geese in the vicinity.

The trail continues past the left side of the lake, climbing steeply up a stony path to above the waterfall. Stay on the left slope until reaching the pass, at around 4600 meters. Just beyond the pass and to the left, a wide pasture opens before you with the peak of *Salkantay Este* behind it.

From the pass to the village of *Quesca* takes two and a half hours of hiking. Follow the trail along the right side of the pasture. At the pasture's edge, the trail descends steeply down the mountainside to some ruins by the stream. The ruins, no more than some overgrown walls and enclosures, appear to have once been an Inca tambo.

From the ruins, follow the trail across the stream and along the left slope of the valley. Remain on this side and take the lowest trail along the slope. You will come to a shelf in the valley floor which emits two waterfalls. Descend to below the shelf and camp at the double waterfalls, some two hours from the pass.

The next morning continue down the valley, walking beneath the line of peaks and glaciers of the Huayanays and following the remains of an Inca road. An hour's descent brings you to the village of *Quesca*. At Quesca the trail splits. Stay to the left and hike past the school before climbing a short distance to the trail on the left slope.

From Quesca, the *Inca Trail* and *Huayllabamba* are a three-hour hike away. Continue down the valley along the left slope. Shortly before the valley joins with the *quebrada Cusichaca,* an Inca road will become evident. The road leads to the ruins of *Paucarcancha.* Covered in weeds and forgotten, the ruins lie off the beaten path of tourism and display the natural state of structures left behind by a dead civilization. Paucarcancha,

Waterfalls provide a perfect backdrop for evening's camp.

meaning Flowery Field, stands above the juncture of two streams and two Inca roads. The trail you have just hiked leads back to Cuzco by way of Chinchero. The other trail runs up the Cusichaca to the pass at Nv. Salkantay.

At the ruins be sure to cross the Cusichaca above the conjunction of the two streams and hike down along its left bank. To follow the trail along the right bank is to take a path of despair amid fields, brush, and brambles.

Huayllabamba lies a half hour downstream from Paucarcancha. You can continue along the Inca Trail, or you can follow the trail down the Cusichaca to Km 88 and take the train back to Cuzco or on to Machu Picchu.

3

Ollantaytambo to Huayllabamba

ELEVATION GAIN: 1832 m
ELEVATION LOSS: 1860 m

LENGTH: 3 days
DISTANCE: 38 km

Ollantaytambo can be another starting point for the Inca Trail, either by following the rio Urubamba to Chilca and on downriver, or by trekking up into the mountains of the Urubamba valley southwest of the town's ruins. The mountain trail, outlined below, not only provides spectacular views of the valley and a chance to see seldom-visited Inca sites but also wends its way over the gently rolling plateau above the rio Urubamba. The hike passes an Inca quarry and a small group of ruins before cresting the valley ridge and linking up with the trail from Chilca (described in the previous section). Because of the extremely steep climbing involved and the high elevations, this trail is more difficult than the two preceding treks.

How to Get There
Although you can take the train from Cuzco to Ollantaytambo, this route will add to your trek an additional two-kilometer walk back upriver. Instead, ride a *colectivo* from Av. Huascar 128 to Urubamba and then to Ollantaytambo by small truck. Get out just before town where the asphalt ends.

The Trek

Begin the trek by crossing to the other side of the rio Urubamba by way of a footbridge. Notice that a modern bridge has been built over the ancient footings of an Inca bridge that once spanned the same spot. Upriver a short distance, a huge boulder sits in midstream where the Incas placed it to divert erosive currents away from the footing.

From the bridge, the trail turns downstream to run beside the numerous terraces along the river's left bank. Just before the train station, the trail gradually begins to ascend the slope. As a rule, keep to the left when the trail forks. As you rise along the slope, the beautiful geometric fields around Ollanta fan across the valley floor.

Rounding a spur in the valley, you enter onto the road from *Cachiqhata,* the quarry site from which the stone for the fortress of Ollanta was taken. Large stone blocks called *piedras cansadas,* literally translated as "tired stones," lie along the path. They were left midway between the quarry and the town when the Spanish invasion prevented the completion of Ollanta.

Continuing up the road you will come to small round burial towers known as *chullpas.* The pre-hispanic people buried their dead in these small cylinders, mummifying and wrapping the bodies before setting them in the fetal position among objects to be used in the afterlife. Despite the efforts of the sixteenth-century church and Spanish monarchy to stop the plundering of these tombs, their decrees did not halt looting of the sacred sites by *hauqueros,* graverobbers. Today, chullpas throughout the Andes and along the coast stand desecrated and empty.

In a curve in the mountainside, various staging areas for the quarrying of the stone still stand. Jean-Pierre Protzen, who has studied the site of Cachiqhata, believes that the Incas did not actually quarry the stone here by exploiting with pry bars the natural faults and cracks in the cliff face as they did at other sites, but instead chose their stone from the peak's rockfall. The laborous process of transporting the huge blocks to the construction site was carried out with the use of many men and llamas, and perhaps with log rollers beneath the stone. One theory states that stones were transported across the rio Urubamba by diverting the river to one side, moving the stone to the center, and then, to complete the crossing, diverting the river to the opposite side.

The shaping of the crude stone blocks is less well-understood, but Professor Protzen believes a method of hitting stone against stone was used to mold them. The Incas used three sizes of chiseling stone — the size depending on whether the block was to be roughly formed for transport or finely finished for placement in a wall. The chiseling rock was held between the hands and then repeatedly dropped in rapid succession against the block. In this way a six-sided block could be fashioned in a relatively short period of time, the professor having finished one such block in less than ninety minutes. Nonetheless, numerous test fittings were still required to match the newly shaped stones to their neighboring blocks before mortarless walls, the trademark of the Incas, could be formed. One fantastical theory that has been around for years, ever since the lost British explorer Colonel Faucett expounded it, conjectures that blocks were made with the use of a jungle plant that dissolved rock. There is no evidence, however, that such a plant ever existed.

The trail continues past a campesino's house, rounds the hill, and passes under a rocky crag. The trail then steeply ascends the valley. Once you come to Mario Santos' house, perched high above the valley, the ruins of *Choquetacca* lie a short distance away. Camp next to the ruins. Water can be found in a cistern just below the house of Sr. Santos. The hike from Ollanta to the ruins takes around five hours. In the distance down-valley, *Nv. Veronica* rises to a height of 5750 meters.

The next morning's hike is the most difficult, since the trail winds nearly straight up the valley side to the gap between the two cliff faces behind the ruins. The hike takes around three hours of arduous climbing. The trail runs directly behind the ruins, twisting and turning its way toward the towering cliff faces. At times, the trail becomes almost indiscernable in the grass and rock, but continues in the direction of the gap. Once you are between the cliffs, the trail continues its snakelike pattern upward before turning to cross the left cliff top.

The hike from the gap to the next camp, located above the village of Ancascocha, takes some three to three and a half hours. After cutting over the cliff top, the trail circles around the back and winds to the right down an open area of rolling hills. In the distance, you can see the pass between the mountains of Salkantay Este and Huayanay. Heading southwest you come to a small village.

The trail continues on the right-hand slope beyond the village. Follow the path over a crest, then descend to a wash. From here, take the trail that runs along the left-hand slope. Do not descend but continue heading up the valley on the level trail high above the stream and valley floor. Only just before the village of *Ancascocha* does the trail begin its descent. Camp just beyond the village of Ancascocha as described in the previous section. The next day follow the route from Ancascocha described in the Chilca to Huayllabamba trek.

The Cordillera Vilcabamba
& Nv. Salkantay

Spreading along an east-west axis, the mountains of the Cordillera Vilcabamba rise to form a ragged chain between the region's two great rivers, the Urubamba and the Apurimac. With the upper valleys of the Apurimac to the south and the jungles of the Urubamba to the north, the Cordillera Vilcabamba is the ultimate hurdle between highland and lowland. Consequently, along the cordillera's northern side, massive snow peaks collide with tropical rain forests to create a brilliant contrast between lush vegetation and lofty desolation.

Because of its geographic location, the range barred the highland inhabitants from the jungle's stores of tropical foods, yet protected them from lowland tribes. Realizing this, the Incas built roads through and along the mountain range both to gain access to the jungle and to better guard against the intrusion of foreign tribes. The Inca Trail was one such road, but many others were also built and are still used today for commerce between the highland and lowland people.

The Cordillera Vilcabamba stands northwest of Cuzco. Nv. Salkantay, the cordillera's tallest peak, is at the eastern end of the chain and rises to 6271 meters in height. The name Salkantay means Savage Mountain, which may refer to the clouds that rise up from the jungle lowlands and engulf the peak. The mountain acts as a hub for valleys spread out around it and for trails crossing its passes. Mollepata, a town that stands far above the deep valley of the Apurimac, is the starting point for the three treks into the upper valleys around Nv. Salkantay described in this section.

4

Mollepata to Huayllabamba

ELEVATION GAIN: 2030 m
ELEVATION LOSS: 2130 m.

LENGTH: 4 days
DISTANCE: 55 km

The first route from Mollepata is a well-known trail that leads the trekker up into some of the most beautiful highland valleys of the region. The trail winds up over a landscape dotted by fields and thatched-roof houses to enter the valley of Soray that cuts up through the mountainous terrain to the very base of Nv. Salkantay. Crossing a pass near 4880 meters, the trail descends over a broad marshy valley floor and finally drops down along the side of a steep quebrada, fording rushing streams to join the Inca Trail at Huayllabamba.

The trail makes the greatest elevation gain of all the treks presented in the guide. Trekkers should be prepared for the long days of climbing involved and the possible accompanying effects of altitude. Because of the elevation gain, you should give yourself adequate time to adjust to high altitude in Cuzco prior to embarking on the trek.

How to Get There

Trucks leave daily to Mollepata between 8 and 9 a.m. from Av. Arcopata, an extension of Calle Montero off Saphi. Be prepared for a bumpy, dusty ride of four to five hours' length.

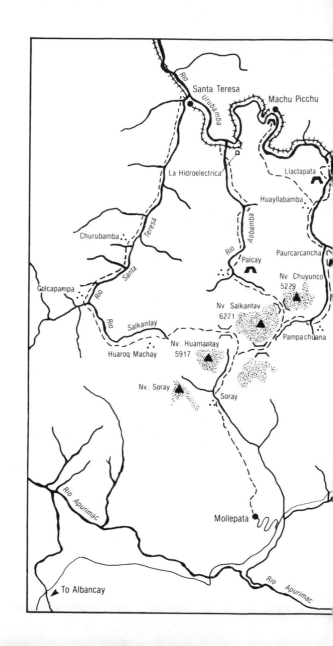

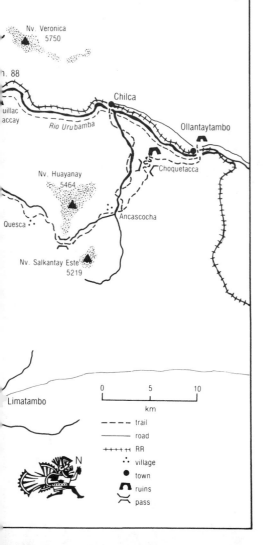

The Cordillera Vilcabamba & Nv. Salkantay

Nv. Veronica
5750

h. 88

uillac
accay

Rio Urubamba

Chilca

Ollantaytambo

Choquetacca

Nv. Huayanay
5464

Quesca

Ancascocha

Nv. Salkantay Este
5219

Limatambo

0   5   10
km

- - - - trail
———— road
+++++ RR
∴ village
● town
⌂ ruins
⌣ pass

N

Luckily for the traveler, the journey is a nature tour in itself. Around the town of Anta, long lines of snowcapped mountains jut up from behind the hills. Then, as the truck descends toward Limatambo, the deep valleys around the rio Apurimac open before you, the shark-toothed Nv. Salkantay standing over the entire scene. Be sure to get a truck direct to Mollepata; otherwise you might have to walk the last eleven steep kilometers from the main road to the town. The trip costs around US $1.50.

The Trek

Since trucks arrive in Mollepata in the early afternoon, you can hike a few hours out of Mollepata on the first day. Walk uphill out of town till you reach a dirt road, which you should follow uphill to the right. After walking twenty to thirty minutes, a horseshoe basin formed by a low ridge will come into view. The trail follows the road until it comes beneath the ridge's lowest point, where a stream runs nearby. You can reach this point by either following the road or taking a path that leads off to the right near a group of houses. Eventually, they will meet again at an irrigation canal. Once you reach the stream that flows down the apex of the basin you should fill your canteens since there is little water near camp. The hike from Mollepata to the stream takes two hours.

A short distance from the stream the trail crosses the aqueduct near a house and doubles back up the ridge, making long switchbacks up the hill through fields and high brush. Just under a cross and before the low point in the ridge, the trail breaks from the road to continue steeply up the hill to the cross. Follow the trail to the right along the crest of the ridge, heading east. One hour from the stream, you will come to pastures where you can camp for the night.

On the second day, you will hike from the pastures to just above the village of Soray, some five hours away. Continue along the trail, walking uphill to the left and toward the northeast. The trail climbs through trees and bushes before crossing to the other side of the hill. Do not descend into the valley below but keep to the steep slope, crossing a spur and finally entering the valley to Soray.

Before you a magnificent peak can be seen. It is not Nv. Salkantay but its brother peak, *Nv. Huamantay* (5917 meters). The gentle ascent up the valley heads north by northwest. Here in the valley, as elsewhere along the trail, hummingbirds dart from flower to flower and from bush to bush. Their inconspicuous size is betrayed only by their iridescent colors. Despite their fragile appearance, hummingbirds *(Trochilidae)* have adapted to a wide range of climatic conditions, enabling them to live in the high altitudes and freezing temperatures that are found around Nv. Salkantay. To survive the Andean nights without starving or moving to lower altitudes, hummingbirds fall into a torpid state where their body temperature hovers just above the ambient temperature and their metabolism slows to one-twentieth of its daytime rate.

Just before *Soray* the valley broadens and flattens. Continue up the center of the valley, and then return to the left side to avoid a marshy plain. You will pass through fields before crossing over a bridge to the right side of the stream. Enter the narrow valley, at the end of which *Nv. Salkantay* looms. Either camp here or continue up a steep slope to a small site just left of the trail. To hike from Soray to the camp in the upper valley requires about one hour.

The hummingbird inhabits the lower valleys around Nv. Salkantay, but the rocky crags and peaks towering above them are the domain of the Andean condor *(Vultur gryphus)*. As the world's largest bird, the Andean condor has a wing span that can reach up to ten feet. Though little is known about the bird, it is believed that some 20,000 live along the length of the Andes. It is also believed that the condor lives for as long as fifty years.

Andean Condor

An immensely ugly bird, this vulture nonetheless has a place on the coats of arms of Bolivia, Chile, Colombia, and Ecuador, and is the national symbol of Peru. Because of the folklore and superstition that surround this huge bird, it also has a place in a particularly brutal ritual of the campesinos. The ritual requires that the campesinos capture a condor, sometimes by waiting days in a pit covered with a rotting carcass. When a wary condor lands atop the pit, they grab its legs and then, once the bird is captured, an *Aywar Fiesta* can be held. For this, the condor is strapped to a bull's back, and the pair released in a ring. As the bull rages about the ring with the condor's razor-sharp beak pecking at its back and the bird's long wings beating the air, the audience cheers from ringside. In some areas, the fiesta is ended by killing the bull and then feeding its heart and some chicha to the condor. The intoxicated bird is finally released. This all takes place to demonstrate the superiority of Indian gods, symbolized by the condor, over foreign ones, represented by the bull — an animal brought to Peru by the Spanish.

Incachiriaska pass lies some four hours from camp. In the morning, follow the stony trail along the right side of the valley towards Nv. Salkantay, and after a half hour you will reach the bank of the stream and a grassy meadow. Before you the scree of glacial moraines winds down the mountain's base like snakes basking in the sun. To the left of the first moraine lies the trail to Santa Teresa. To the right runs the trail to Incachiriaska and Huayllabamba.

Cross the stream and, staying right, follow the trail to the foot of the moraine. The trail then makes its way along the right slope of the valley. Climb the steep slope to an area covered with tough, spiky clumps of *ichu* grass. The trail heads directly towards Nv. Salkantay, climbing to the right of the cliffs that face the moraine. The trail then crosses the tops of these cliffs, and continues running parallel to the moraine before reaching rocky crags and large boulders.

The trail now turns right, heading to the east. Continue along the right slope over the grassy hills. At a ravine where a stream comes dripping down from a mossy embankment,

Nv. Salkantay's southern face looks down on Soray pampa.

cross to the left side of the ravine. Hike across a rolling knoll, keeping to the right-hand slope. Do not cross over the moraine toward the mountain. The pass lies to the east between two rocky crags and is formed of loose gravel and large stones. The hundred meters of trail before the top of the pass runs over this rocky ground. Tall stone piles mark the trail at intervals.

Once arriving at *Incachiriaska,* which lies at 4880 meters, you can look west and see the pass that leads to Santa Teresa and the jungle. From Incachiriaska, the trail heads east down through a long, broad valley to *Pampachuana,* a village some four hours away. The trail descends the pass on the right. Once in the valley, it passes corrals and other structures. Stay to the right. The trail then crosses to the stream's left side and remains here till Pampachuana. It is best to camp above Pampachuana since there are few campsites in the narrow valley past the village.

The morning of the fourth day you hike to the village. Here you will see that the Incas canalized the stream for five hundred meters. Near the canal's end, cross to the right side. From Pampachuana, it takes around three hours to hike down the narrow, steep valley to *Huayllabamba*. A half hour above Huayllabamba, you will come to the fortress ruins of *Paucarcancha*. This is a site worth exploring, but be careful not to climb on the walls or to do anything else that might damage the structures.

At Paucarcancha, the trail crosses a bridge to the left bank of the stream, then continues on to Huayllabamba, where you can enter on the Inca Trail or walk to the train station at Km 88, three hours farther down the valley. Trains to Cuzco leave daily at around 9:30 a.m. and 5:30 p.m. Trains to Machu Picchu head in the opposite direction and come about an hour earlier than the Cuzco trains. There are no afternoon trains on Sundays.

5

Mollepata to Santa Teresa

ELEVATION GAIN: 1850 m
ELEVATION LOSS: 3190 m

LENGTH: 5 days
DISTANCE: 65 km

Of all the treks in the Cuzco area, a hike from Mollepata to Santa Teresa best exhibits the Andes' distinct ecosystems spread across its different zones of altitude and climate. The trail climbs from the temperate high valleys around the rio Apurimac to the sparsely inhabited puna around Nv. Salkantay, then descends into the lush valleys northwest of the mountain. The unique diversity of the landscape derives from the variance in environmental factors — sun, water, temperature, soil — that occurs along the rise of a high-altitude region in a tropical part of the world. The ecosystems transform rapidly from one climatic and altitudinal zone to another: banana plantations replace potato fields, and dull-brown mountain viscachas give way to colorful green parrots.

The Trek

Follow the instructions given in the previous section regarding transportation and your first two days of hiking. In the meadow above *Soray,* the trail to *Santa Teresa* branches off the Huayllabamba trail at the foot of the moraine. Cross over the meadow to the left side of the valley. At the foot of the moraine the trail climbs steeply up a wash before switchbacking up the valley's left side.

At the end of the switchbacks, the trail follows along the slope and then crosses a stream. Continue toward the pass by walking between the stream and the moraine. Just before the pass, the trail resumes climbing the left slope. The second night's camp and the pass are only about three hours apart.

The pass stands at approximately 4700 meters and is marked by a number of apachetas, stones piled together. Traditionally, a traveler will take a stone with him at the start of his journey. Once attaining the pass, he adds his stone to an existing pile for good luck and strength. A type of huaca, the apecheta is considered sacred.

The trail continues down the opposite side of the pass through rocky terrain. Stay to the left slope until finally reaching the broad pastures of *Huaroq Machay,* some two and a half hours from the pass. Camp here for the night.

On the fourth day, you continue down the valley of the rio Salkantay to its juncture with the rio Santa Teresa near the village of *Colcapampa.* The trail remains on the left slope as the valley narrows and becomes heavily vegetated. You are entering the *ceja de selva,* literally "the brow of the jungle." The low puna grass is replaced by bushes, and soon trees and bamboo become evident. Even at this altitude I happened to see a flock of noisy, bright-green parrots flying from tree to tree.

After three to four hours of hiking, you cross the rio Santa Teresa above Colcapampa. Continue down the left side of the Santa Teresa toward the next camp, which is two hours away at *Churubamba.* A half hour below Colcapampa, the trail leads to a stream and then continues on the opposite side some thirty meters upstream. Farther on, you will come to a beautiful waterfall. Next to the trail at Churubamba there is a grassy area for camping, though you may choose to continue walking

Apachetas line Nv. Salkantay's western pass.

another forty minutes to a campsite just past a large stream and house at *Playa*.

The final day of the trek is spent walking six to seven hours to *Santa Teresa* at the end of the valley. The trail, passing by coffee and banana plantations, stays on the left slope all the way to this jungle town. The last hour and a half before town the path turns to a dirt road. In Santa Teresa (1510 meters), you'll find accommodations for the night. Trains leave for Cuzco morning, afternoon, and night.

6

Mollepata to La Hidroelectrica

ELEVATION GAIN: 2030 m   LENGTH: 5-6 days
ELEVATION LOSS: 3152 m   DISTANCE: 65 km

The trek from Mollepata to La Hidroelectrica is the interior route of the three routes around Nv. Salkantay. The Palcay trek, as it is known, combines several distinct features of the two outlying treks. Like the trek to Santa Teresa, this route winds through the jungle regions above the rio Urubamba and, like the trek to Huayllabamba, passes an Inca ruin and the remnants of an Inca road. It terminates at the power station on the rio Urubamba, with the ruins of Machu Picchu lying just a short train and bus ride away. The Palcay trek is the most difficult of the three hikes because it leads over two of Nv. Salkantay's passes before dropping into the jungle.

The Trek
The first three days of the hike are the same as those of the Mollepata-to-Huayllabamba trek and should be followed as described in that section. After Incachiriaska, camp at the foot of the mountain's lowest moraine, two hours below the pass.

On the morning of the fourth day, you must ascend to the pass between Nv. Salkantay and Nv. Chuyunco. It lies some one and a half to two hours above the valley floor. The trailhead to Palcay begins just below the moraines, and climbs along the grassy slope parallel to Nv. Salkantay's stony veins. The grass thins and becomes loose stone as the trail begins to switchback to the pass, which you arrive at after climbing beyond a narrow slot in the ridge between Nv. Salkantay and Nv. Chuyunco.

From the pass, you can see a broad pasture unfolding below you. The trail leads off to the right before once again switchbacking down to the pasture. Cross the pasture, picking up the trail at its far end. The trail then descends along the left slope of the valley. It is where the valley curves to the left that you can see where the *rio Aobamba* begins its course to the rio Urubamba.

The ruins of Palkay lie some four to five hours from the pass. Continue down the valley, staying to the left of the Aobamba. You cross a rock-strewn wash before switch-backing down into an area with orchids in the trees and along the ground. Be sure to close any gates you open.

Down the trail, a valley opens to your left. Here a hanging valley emits two waterfalls. Directly across from this valley on the opposite bank of the Aobamba stand the ruins of *Palcay.* Just above the valley's stream, a trail crosses the river and makes its way to the ruins.

Palkay was once an outpost for Machu Picchu. It is similar in construction to the sites found along the Inca Trail and was connected to them by a road. The road has fallen into disuse, isolating these ruins from the ones along the Inca Trail.

Recross the river and descend to two houses. Make camp in one of the grassy areas near the river, or continue down the valley to pastures an hour away.

To hike to *la Hidroelectrica,* on the rio Urubamba, takes some eight hours to complete, and winds much of the way through dense jungle growth. Begin below the village by crossing over a bridge to the right side of the river, where a wall of trees and bushes rises abruptly before you. This marks the beginning of vegetation that will grow ever the more dense as you descend the valley.

Entering into the forest, you can see the faint outlines and remains of an Inca road. Just after you pass the pastures for camping, you cross another bridge back to the left bank. The path is easily followed down through bamboo groves and into forests of increasingly taller trees. There are no settlements until a short distance above the power station. For hours, you walk through jungle that has been left almost untouched by man; it is in marked contrast to the jungle along the rio Santa Teresa, where houses and plantations dot the length of the valley. Along the rio Aobamba, the dense jungle gives up only a few areas suitable for camping. If you are going to camp in the jungle, look for a site well before sunset.

The Aobamba valley harbors an abundance of bird and animal life. Once while I was passing through a heavily wooded area along the trail, I heard rustling in a nearby tree. Looking up, my gaze was returned by dark eyes peering from a brown furry face. In the branch above clung a *coati,* a raccoonlike animal typical of tropical South America. The coati is about the same size as a raccoon, and also has a similar ringed tail. His face, however, differed; it exhibited a long pointed snout and lacked the bandit mask of his North American cousin.

Coca is cultivated in humid tropical valleys throughout the jungle regions of Peru and Bolivia. Commonly used by campesinos, the leaf of the coca plant is chewed with lime to release a mild narcotic effect. The consumption of leaves should not be confused with the use of cocaine, which, though derived from the leaves, is a highly refined and processed chemical product of the plant.

Because of the coca leaf's long history in the Andes, myths and rituals abound relating to its use. The Inca nobility, wanting to reserve the use of coca for themselves, banned it from the Andean masses. It was not until the colonial period that the leaf came into widespread use. Propagated by the Spanish, the numbing leaf helped alleviate the hunger and suffering of abused laborers. Today, the leaf serves a wide variety of purposes, from brewing it for mate, a cure-all tea comparable to chicken soup, to burning it as an offering to apus and Pachamama. It is even used as a remedy for headaches: leaves are wetted with saliva and then stuck to the sufferer's temples.

Legend recounts that Mama Coca was a beautiful woman of extreme sexual desires. As a result of her promiscuous excesses, Mama Coca was put to death and her body cut to pieces and scattered throughout the land, whereby coca bushes sprang up in their place. In memory of the diety, a man could not remove coca leaves from his *chuspa,* a woven carrying pouch, until he made love to a woman. Perhaps because of the widespread and frequent use of the leaf today this honorarium has fallen out of strict practice.

Approximately five hours before the power station, a bridge takes you to the right bank and is followed by another one that crosses a stream entering the river. Continuing northwest, you cross to the left bank of the Aobamba shortly before the station to avoid the cascade of water vented from the right hillside, which forms part of the project. Once reaching the railroad tracks, follow them up the Urubamba valley to la Hidroelectrica.

To avoid confusion, it is best to make your presence known to the police who guard the area. Trains heading toward Cuzco and Machu Picchu pass through the area around 8:30 a.m. and 3:30 p.m.

The Cordillera Vilcanota
& Nv. Ausangate

A clear day in Cuzco reveals the shining white massif of Nv. Ausangate to the southeast of the city. The peak stands like a sentinel over the Cuzco valley, its 6372-meter height surpassing that of all other peaks in the region. Surrounding Nv. Ausangate are the jagged peaks of the Cordillera Vilcanota, a range of mountains clustered together to form rugged hiking territory and vistas of startling beauty.

Within the valleys of the Cordillera Vilcanota live an abundance of animals, both wild and domesticated. Vicuñas roam freely over the rolling hills, and nearly every highland bird, from the giant coot with its comic oversized feet to the predatory mountain caracara, can be found in the skies and on the lakes of the area. Also, huge herds of tame llamas and alpacas graze in the broad valleys.

The campesinos who live in the shadows of the mountains go about their lives in a manner that has altered little over hundreds of years. As speakers of Quechua, they know little or no Spanish. They tend their herds and plant fields of potatoes, the only crop that can survive the altitude's bitter elements. At best, their contact with the world beyond their villages and valleys remains limited.

In their isolation from the man-made world of towns and cities, the people of the region identify closely with the natural world around them. The land and the spirits inhabiting it play a powerful role in the lives of the people. The greatest spirit of them all is Apu Ausangate, a diety that dwells in the mountain's highest region and is the subject of countless tales. One legend recounts how the apu intervened in a war between Peru and Chile. Soldiers from both armies were assembled near the peak, but the Peruvians were hopelessly outmatched. The people of the area asked for the apu's aid, and in reply he sent down lightning bolts that struck Chilean soldiers dead. The foreign army retreated in terror, leaving the Peruvians, for once, victorious.

7

The Ausangate Circuit

ELEVATION GAIN: 1270 m   LENGTH: 4-6 days
ELEVATION LOSS: 1270 m   DISTANCE: 80 km

A hike around the base of Nv. Ausangate contains both spectacular mountain scenery and highland animal life. Unsurprisingly, the Ausangate Circuit has become a popular hike, one that is possible to complete in a week or as little time as four days. Not only does the trail circle Nv. Ausangate, but it also passes numerous other snowcapped peaks and ice-cold lakes nestled at the mountain's foot. It comes within earshot of the mountain's massive glaciers, enabling you to hear the slabs of ice as they crack, crumble, and finally crash to the waters below. Then, in the valleys west of the peak, the trail passes huge herds of alpacas and llamas grazing peacefully. Amid this natural beauty, you can also enjoy the luxury of a relaxing bath in the hot springs that are found at both the beginning and the end of the trek.

How to Get There

Plan on a day's travel to get to Tinqui, which is located just beyond the town of Ocongate. Trucks leave for Ocongate from below Mercado Huanchac, at the corner of Av. Pachacutec and Huascar. On Mondays, Wednesdays, and Fridays, trucks depart for Ocongate between 10:00 and 11:00 a.m. On Tuesdays, Thursdays, and Sundays, trucks return from Ocongate. On Saturdays, trucks leave early for Cuzco and sometimes return to Ocongate in the afternoons. The trip takes around six hours; much of it is over rough, dirt road. From Ocongate, catch a truck in the plaza to Tinqui, thirty minutes farther down the road. The fare from Cuzco to Tinqui should be around US $2.

It is possible to reach Tinqui from Cuzco on an off-day. Take an early bus from Av. Tacna off of Av. Garcilaso de la Vega to Urcos, where you should wait in the plaza until a truck to Ocongate, Quince Mil, or Puerto Maldonado arrives to pick up passengers.

The Trek

The trail from *Tinqui* to the village of *Upis* runs over hilly pampa and takes three to four hours to hike. Begin by crossing the bridge near the soccer field. Walk five hundred meters over a slight rise to a second bridge and stream. Crossing the bridge, you follow the trail to the right, up the hill, and past a row of houses.

Beyond the houses sits a large boulder deposited on the pampa by glacial movements. The trail divides and heads in many directions here. Continue along a trail that leads between two lines of dirt fencing. To get to Upis, you walk in the direction of Nv. Ausangate's visible glacier, heading southeast by compass. Follow the depressions, fence lines, and small trails across several rises in the pampa. The area is well-populated, so if you are uncertain of your course you can ask for directions.

While hiking through the spiky ichu grass of the pampa, you may see an Andean gull *(Larus serranus)* hovering on the winds. The marshes and small ponds around Upis provide a perfect habitat for the bird. This gull has a thin white body and a black head. In the winter, however, the black plumage can change to almost pure white.

Just before *Upis* you will enter a broad valley heading toward the glacier. Walk up this valley along its left slope. Do not descend onto the valley floor because it is quite swampy and only necessitates hopscotching from one clump of marsh grass to another. The village of Upis stands on the left slope and overlooks a rounded pasture. Continue up the valley to the *hot springs* twenty minutes away. Camp here for the night, or hike another three hours to the next campsite near the lakes of Pucacocha.

The first time I camped at the base of Nv. Ausangate I had to huddle in my sleeping bag to keep warm as a light May snow fell outside the tent. The mountain was hidden in fog, and its crags would momentarily loom from behind the fog before once again vanishing inside the misty cloak. In the lexicon of mountains and their apus, Nv. Ausangate holds special significance for the campesinos of the area. It is in the frozen heights of the peak that condemned souls of murderers and incestuous persons are doomed to wander. Sentenced to climb naked to the mountain's top for absolution of their sins, the condemned are eternally engaged in this Sisyphean task, because they near the peak only to be repeatedly blown back down by fierce winds. In the hostile weather of that first night, I could hardly think of a more appropriate inferno for those lost souls. With my tent rattling in the wind, I dozed off uneasily, hoping not to have any midnight visitors.

On the next day, hike some two hours to the ridge between Nv. Ausangate and *Nv. Queullacocha.* Continue up the valley along the right slope before climbing a rock-strewn area that lies between the two peaks. A hut and a few corrals form the last settlement you'll come across before you climb toward the mountain. Follow the fenceline and cross to the far slope. Heading in a southwesterly direction, cross the ridge by walk-

122

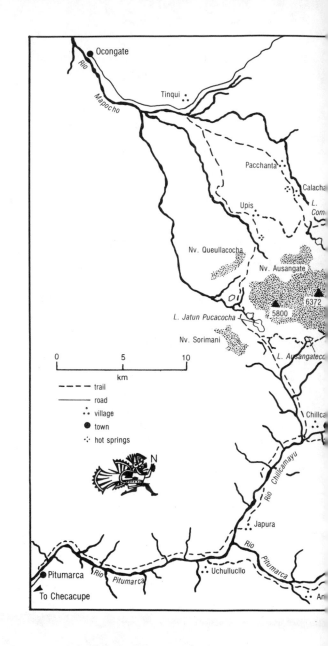

The Cordillera Vilcanota
& Nv. Ausangate

Puca Punta

▲ Senal Nv. Tres Picos

ta Catalina   Qampa

L. Sibinacocha

Sallma

Nv. Chuallani ▲

Rio Chuamayu

Canchapampa

Yanamayu

L. Aereacocha

ing to the left of the steep hill between it and Nv. Ausangate.

The ridge forms a broad, rolling bridge between the two peaks. The trail runs to the left along Nv. Ausangate's slope. Do not descend into the valley on the opposite side or climb any farther. Crossing a stream, continue along the steep left slope. The trail circles around the rocky crags of the mountain to the ponds above the Pucacocha lakes. You can set up camp here.

Laguna Jatun Pucacocha, an hour and a half away from the upper ponds, is the second night's campsite. Follow the trail past the ponds before descending steeply along a stream, past *Laguna Vinococha* and toward a waterfall in the distance. The trail climbs along the left side of the waterfall before crossing at its top to the right side. The trail continues to the right before running between a rock knoll and the spired heights of *Nv. Sorimani.* Hike past *Laguna Huchuy Pucacocha,* again crossing between rock knoll and mountains to reach the highest and largest of the three lakes, Laguna Jatun Pucacocha. Camp at the lake's shore.

The waters of the lakes harbor a variety of birds. Waterfowl such as Andean geese, giant coots, and ducks paddle about upon the water's surface. It was on the lake's shore, however, that I first saw the mountain caracara *(Phalcobaenus albogularis),* known as an *akche* in Quechua. I watched the caracara scavenge along the shore, its black plumage and white underside standing out amid the dull highland colors. Its unmistakable markings — yellow-orange legs and a red fold of skin at the beak — distinguish it from other birds. Living above 3000 meters, the mountain caracara feeds on small animals, reptiles, and carrion. A scarcity of such food in the Andes often pits the aggressive caracara against the condor for rights to a carcass.

On the third day, you can either walk toward the mountains south of Nv. Ausangate and head to Pitumarca, or you can

Caracara

continue around the peak. To continue the circuit, leave camp by heading east over a rock knoll. Stay to the right slope and cross the first ravine at its top. You will come to a second ravine where you must make a crossing wherever possible. Then hike to a large round boulder in the distance. You will continue to ascend between the red bluffs of *Cerro Ausangate Apacheta* and Nv. Ausangate. After hiking an hour and a half, you will come to a high hillside that overlooks the waters of *Laguna Ausangatecocha.* Descend to the lake, from which it is a two-hour climb to the first pass, lying at 5070 meters. Circle to the right of the lake, following along the stream that runs at the side of the moraine. Above the moraine, you cut sharply to the right and ascend along the crest of a spur. The pass is at the far left-hand side between the rocky crags of Nv. Ausangate and a hill in the ridge.

From the pass, you can descend to the valley floor in an hour's time. Keep to the right of the large ravine and then follow the trail as it loops across the steep slope. Reaching a spur, descend along its crest to the valley floor. Camp in the valley for the night.

On the fourth day, head down the valley to its juncture with the larger valley of the *Chillcamayu*. After turning left up this new valley, you pass corrals and herds of llamas and alpacas. Climb over the hilly terrain and circle left around the marshy areas to reach the upper level of the valley. As you walk up the valley, the peaks of *Señal Nv. Tres Picos* come into sight. A vast icefield lies to their left, and *Nv. Puca Punta* borders the field's opposite side.

Viscacha

The stream flowing through the upper valley is called the *rio Qampamayu.* As you progress up along its left side, you will come to scree. Amid these rocks and bounders, you may spot mountain viscachas *(Lagidium peruanum),* animals related to the chinchilla and who live in warrens among the rocks. Muted brown in color, this rodent has long ears and a long tail, and looks like a cross between a rabbit and a giant gerbil. The mountain viscacha was never sought for its fur as its cousin the chinchilla was, but it is hunted for food.

You will come to the village of *Qampa* some two hours after the juncture of the two valleys. At the village, the trail turns left and heads up through broken terrain before crossing a bridge and reaching a marshy pasture. In front of you lies the icefield. The pass, however, lies to the left of the icefield in a corridor between *Nv. Puca Punta* and the mountain mass of Nv. Ausangate. You cannot see the pass until you have begun the final ascent. Do not attempt to cross the pass unless you have good weather and enough daylight to make it to camp, which lies several hours below the crest. If you don't have either one of these, camp above the pasture.

From Qampa to the *pass* takes around two and a half to three hours to hike. From the pasture, climb up the left slope, past corrals and conical-shaped dung bins. The trail heads in a northwesterly direction and then, as you turn west, continues through the long corridor that forms the pass. The trail climbs steeply up the stony rubble before working its way along a shelf.

Once you reach the pass, you can see an *icecave* in the ravine below. It leads into the glacier of Nv. Puca Punta and, if you have both the time and the energy, is worth exploring. The trail from the pass down to *Laguna Comercocha* takes between one and a half to two hours to cover. Hike down the left slope. Two lakes will come into sight off to the right. You should cross the small pasture before the first lake, but do not head in the direction of the lake. Instead, follow the trail over the ridge that borders the lake on its left. The trail then crosses the hills beside the two lakes before descending to the third and largest lake, Laguna Comercocha, and camp.

The next morning, follow the trail down the valley, keeping to the left-hand slope. The valley broadens and turns to the right. Here you must ford a stream to continue down the left slope. Two hours from the lake, you will come to the village of *Calachaca,* shortly beyond which lie a hot spring and pools for bathing.

After this first village, you will come to a village with a schoolhouse. This is *Pacchanta.* From Pacchanta to *Tinqui* is a two- to two-and-a-half-hour hike. The trail leaves the village by way of a road that is under construction on the valley's left slope and on the nearby hills. Once you reach the sloping plain of the hills, a well-worn track runs several kilometers down the gentle slope before reaching Tinqui.

Transportation from Tinqui to Ocongate and Cuzco has no definite schedule, but at least a few trucks a day run in that direction. We once arrived in Tinqui at 3:30 in the afternoon and caught a truck to Ocongate within half an hour. By nightfall we were on our way to Cuzco. The truck ride was like a mobile slumber party, with everyone feeling like old friends. To soften the bumpy ride, songs were sung and stories exchanged. We rolled into Cuzco at 2:00 a.m., then all headed to more stable beds.

8

Tinqui to Pitumarca

ELEVATION GAIN: 1100 m   LENGTH: 4 days
ELEVATION LOSS: 1430 m   DISTANCE: 70 km

The Tinqui-to-Pitumarca trek follows along the Ausangate-circuit route before turning south away from the mountain to head down the populous valleys of the rios Chillcamayu and Pitumarca. This valley system provides a thoroughfare for campesinos on their way to and from the market town of Pitumarca. Caravans of brightly decorated llamas with tassels and bells hung around their necks slowly wend their way along the path. Burdened by sacks and invariably distracted to grazing, the llamas must be continually herded, shooed, and pushed up the trail by campesinos.

Although the trail avoids the two passes on the circuit that are over 5000 meters, it still climbs to above 4900 meters. The valley trail is wide and well-traveled, making this trek less strenuous and less demanding than the circuit.

The Trek
Follow the directions for transportation and the first two days of hiking as given in the previous section as far as the camp at *Laguna Jatun Pucacocha.* On the third day, follow the trail along the foot of the steeple-peaked *Nv. Sorimani* and *Nv.*

Tacusiri mountain group. At the final rocky crag, the trail ascends to the pass between this mountain group and *Cerro Ausangate Apacheta.* Heading southeast along the slope, the trail climbs steeply through a wash before switchbacking to the 4900-meter pass, an hour from the previous night's camp.

The trail then descends through a wide valley to its junction with the *rio Chillcamayu* three hours from the pass. Follow a broad wash in the middle of the valley's upper plateau. In the lower valley, the trail continues to the left of the stream. Numerous llamas and alpacas graze here and are watched over by herdsmen, one of whom I once saw playing a *quena.* The quena is an Andean flute fashioned from bamboo or, more recently, plastic pipe.

Campsites can be found easily in this valley or almost anywhere along the trail running down the Chillcamayu. A knoll at the juncture of the two valleys offers one final view of beautiful Nv. Ausangate before the trail heads into the deep valley toward Pitumarca. Remember that whenever you camp near a village, do so at a distance from the village and with the permission of the villagers.

Potato fields cover the steep slopes of the lower valley near the Chillcamayu. Cultivated in Andean soil for over eight thousand years, potato crops can be grown at altitudes of over 4000 meters and can even survive when planted near the 5000-meter-high snowline. The potato has been an integral part of Peruvian life for millenniums, and no meal is complete without a potato or two, or four, or even more. The Quechua language has a lexicon of over one thousand words to describe the various types of Andean potatoes, and five hundred different types of potato exist in the Cuzco region alone. The Incas measured time by how long it took potatoes to cook, and even used them for divination: an odd number of potatoes was a bad omen, and an even number of the tuber foretold favorable occurrences. Introduced to Europe only after the Conquest, the potato has become a main staple throughout the world. Though the mother of french fries and potato chips, the lowly spud is actually quite rich in nutrients. Today, the value of the world's annual potato harvest surpasses the ransom of gold and silver paid by the Inca Atahualpa to Pizarro.

At the juncture of the two valleys, the trail descends the rio Chillcamayu to the town of *Pitumarca,* some thirty kilometers and seven to eight hours away. Cross the bridge at the end of the stream and continue down along the river's right bank. After a long, open field, cross a bridge to the left bank. You climb and descend a long series of steps before passing the village of Japura. Just after the village, you cross again to the right bank at the first bridge you come to. The main trail remains on the left but leads to a collapsed bridge several hundred meters farther on. So once you cross to the right bank, remain on that side till you reach the town of Pitumarca.

Numerous settlements line the trail. Women of the area distinguish themselves from other regions by wearing broad, oval hats that look similar to those of Chinamen. Distinguishing a person's tribe and home by the hat he or she wears is a custom that dates back prior to the Incas. The Inca decreed that each conquered tribe should retain its distinctive headdress. *Chullos,* Andean knit caps with earflaps, are customarily worn by the men of the Vilcanota region; their chullos are distinguished from others by the intricate designs of beads sewn on them. In the markets of Cuzco, Pisac, Ollantaytambo, and Chinchero, you can notice a variety of headdresses all denoting the origin of their wearers.

You will come to where the Chillcamayu joins the *rio Pitumarca.* Shortly after this point, you will climb above the river's canyon to the summit, which is marked by a cross that coincidentally also marks the halfway point down the valley.

Torrent Duck

You continue on past villages and fields before the narrow valley opens onto a broad plain an hour and a half before Pitumarca.

As you walk along the river bank, you may glimpse torrent ducks rapidly winging their way above the water's course. You might even be so lucky as to see the fowl at work in the rushing white currents from which the bird derives its name. The torrent duck *(Merganetta armata)* makes its home beside swift-flowing rivers where, using its long, stiff tail as a rudder, it bobs in and out of the white water in search of food. It has a narrow red bill set against a white head and neck, while its crown and the back of its neck are black. A striking black line also extends downward from its eye. The rest of its body is grayish-brown in color. Campesinos call the duck *mayuchulla.*

In Pitumarca (pop. 5000), informal accommodations can be arranged for the night. Trucks to Cuzco leave daily between 8:00 and 9:00 a.m. Thereafter, service is infrequent and irregular. At Checacupe, seven kilometers beyond Pitumarca, there is train and bus service in the mornings and afternoons. From Pitumarca to Cuzco is four hours by truck and costs around US $1.

9

Pitumarca to Laguna Sibinacocha

ELEVATION GAIN: 1530 m   LENGTH: 7-8 days
ELEVATION LOSS: 1530 m (to Pitumarca) DISTANCE: 145 km
                1300 m   (to Tinqui)   160 km

Beginning at the town of Pitumarca and following along a
river of the same name, this trek leads to Laguna Sibinacocha,
a fifteen-kilometer-long lake southeast of Nv. Ausangate. As
the trail climbs from the river's deep valley to the rolling puna,
fields of crops are replaced by herds of llamas and alpacas.
Hidden amid the rolling hills, the immense waters of Laguna
Sibinacocha, at 4868 meters above sea level, lie nestled in a
banana-shaped trough bordered on the north by snowy peaks.
From the lake, the trek continues by way of two passes above
5000 meters to the Chillcamayu valley. From here, you can
either return to Pitumarca or head toward Nv. Ausangate and
complete the last portion of the circuit by ending at Tinqui.

Although the trek crosses only two passes and leads
through gently sloping valleys, much of it still runs across terrain above 4800 meters. The high altitudes, coupled with the
trek's duration and remoteness, make it the most challenging
of all the hikes around Cuzco. Hikers should be well accustomed to the Andean backcountry before embarking on this
trek.

How to Get There

To reach Pitumarca from Cuzco, you can choose from three forms of transportation: train, bus, or truck. The train leaves from the Huanchac terminal twice a day except Sundays. The train takes around four hours to reach the small town of Checacupe, seven kilometers southwest of Pitumarca.

Two companies run buses almost hourly between Cuzco and Sicuani, with the ride to Checacupe lasting about three hours. You can purchase tickets for around US $1 from either Empresa Transportes Sur Oriente at Huascar 248 or Empresa Transportes Sol Andino at Pachacutec 413, both located near the Huanchac terminal.

A truck that leaves in the early afternoons from below the San Pedro market runs direct to Pitumarca. Although the cheapest of the three, it is also the most uncomfortable and slowest, taking four to five hours to arrive in Pitumarca.

It is best to leave Cuzco in the afternoon so that you can camp at Pitumarca and get an early start the next morning. If you choose to take the train or bus, you can either walk the seven kilometers from Checacupe to Pitumarca, or take a truck from the town's plaza leaving in the late afternoon. The walk was extremely rewarding for us. Not only were we surrounded by magnificent scenery as we made our way through the valley, but a large flock of green parrots occupying a field adjacent to the road captured our attention. Noisily crying out, they would take to the air from a treetop and, as wings flashed in the sun, they would circle the field. After making several passes, the birds would once again return to a tree only to start the entire colorful process over.

The Trek

Begin in Pitumarca by crossing the river to its left bank and heading up the valley. You will pass houses and fields in the broad valley before it narrows. Continue up the valley along the left side of the river to the village of *Uchullucllo,* four hours from Pitumarca. Just before the village you pass through an area of rock that has eroded into twisted pinnacles and other eerie shapes.

As we walked up the rio Pitumarca, we happened upon two men fishing the river's currents with circular nets. Standing on rocks, they cast their outstretched nets into the waters rushing beneath them. Several stones weighted the perimeter of a net, so when the man pulled up on a line connected to the net's center, the stones closed together beneath the prey, effectively enveloping it in the net. Using these contraptions, the two men were having good luck at pulling fish from the river.

Uchullucllo lies on the other side of the river and practically atop some hot springs. Cross over to the village by using a natural bridge formed of rock hung with stalactites. Walk to the schoolhouse, the only metal-roofed structure in the village. Across the courtyard from the school the trail climbs the slope and heads toward the village of *Anaiso* three hours away.

The trail winds along a series of spurs above the river valley, then cuts to the right across a ridge before once again joining the rio Pitumarca. After crossing the ridge, the trail descends toward the serrated gorge of the river. The tops of these cliffs have been cultivated to the very brink of their dropoffs. The village of Anaiso stands just beyond the gorge where the river meanders across a broad, flat valley. Pass through the village and camp upriver near a stream.

The next day, follow the trail up the valley. It rises steadily on a twisting course until it comes to the highland puna and camp at *Laguna Aereacocha.* When we hiked this route, we found another group of fishermen, this time small boys with long poles for rods. The poles were proving to be less effective than the nets, but the boys didn't mind. Wearing beat-up felt hats and woolen pants that reached to just below their knees, the boys reminded me of Huckleberry Finn and Tom Sawyer transported from the Mississippi River and set down by the rio Pitumarca.

As we walked by them, one of their group offered us a gift of *chuño.* Chuño is made by freeze-drying a small, bitter-tasting potato. Prepared during the winter months of June through August, the potatoes are first put in streams to leach out some of the bitter flavor. Afterward they are placed on the ground where the cold air freezes them during the night. At daybreak campesinos then stomp on them to extract moisture. This process of freezing and stomping repeated over and over finally yields a dried potato that is eaten whole or ground into an easily stored powder. Since chuño could keep for years, the Incas kept large amounts of it in storehouses in case of famine and to feed their armies.

From above Anaiso, you continue up the right side of the broad valley to where it narrows. Cross a bridge to the left side, and follow the wide path through a narrow canyon, fording the river twice. The canyon opens onto a cultivated area. The path then crosses the river once again, climbing up the valley's right-hand slope, and finally arrives at a broad, marshy plain, four hours above the previous night's camp.

You are no longer following the course of the rio Pitumarca. The river now bears the name *rio Yanamayu,* Black River. Just as the waters of the rio Vilcanota are called the rio Urubamba below Calca, the upper portion of the rio Pitumarca has been mysteriously given a different name. Hike across the marshy plain to the upper end, where a small settlement stands. Do not enter the settlement, but cross the river to its left side. The trail then curves to the left, heading east over a spur in the valley. Coming off a steep slope, the trail splits and runs along both sides of the river. Stay to the left side and continue up the valley, remaining near the watercourse. The settlement of *Canchapampa* lies two and a half hours away from the lower end of the marshy plain.

Laguna Aereacocha is another hour and a half away on a plateau above 4800 meters. The trail leaves Canchapampa

Vicuña

heading to the left out of the village. A short distance from the village, the trail cuts across a streambed to the right and heads in an easterly direction over rolling hills. Camp at the lake.

The next day you complete the final leg of the trip to *Laguna Sibinacocha* in three to four hours. Continue across the plateau before descending onto a vast plain laced with rivers. Follow a road leading over the ridge that lies to the east. Once over the ridge, the road turns north and heads to the southern end of Laguna Sibinacocha.

Vicuñas roam this highland region in groups that number anywhere from three to twenty. On this trek, I was able to spot over fifty of the delicate animals. These keen-eyed creatures, however, always observed me first. A shrill, high-pitched warning cry, almost a laugh, would alert me to one's presence. Sometimes, the usually shy vicuña would be gripped by curiosity, and we would watch each other from a distance. Finally tiring of me, it would race away across the puna. The vicuña can reach speeds of up to thirty miles an hour, a remarkable feat at this altitude.

The smallest of the Andean llamoid family, the vicuña *(Vicugña vicugña)* has a small, long neck and a slender build. Soft brown in color, shading to white underneath, the vicuña's fur is the finest in the world, finer than silk. Because of its fur, the species was almost hunted to extinction not too long ago. Hunting vicuna is now illegal, and trading in its pelts brings stiff penalties.

The Inca wore garments woven from only the wool of vicuña. The weaving of these fine clothes, which the Inca would wear just once before ordering them burned, was one of the principal tasks of the Virgins of the Sun. In order to supply the virgins with wool, great hunting parties were assembled in the countryside. Thousands of Indians would first encircle an area and then, as they beat the brush, would come together, tightening the circle until all the game within it was driven into corrals. Though deer and other animals were taken for food, the vicuñas were shorn and released.

Stay to the lake's west side as you walk along the shore. To traverse the length of the lake, you need between four and five hours. Spend a day camped at the lake exploring its shores and the nearby hills and mountains. The lake and its surroundings provide ideal habitat for numerous species of birds. You will see Andean gulls swarm up from the lake's surface in noisy protest of your approach. Giant coots *(Fulica gigantea),* small, black, and resembling a hen with a crimson duck bill, have left their enormous footprints in the sand, and Andean geese waddle and coo along the shoreline. There are numer-

Giant Coot

Alpaca

Llama

ous places to camp, but the lake's northern end offers the spectacular scenery of white peaks.

When you do depart from Laguna Sibinacocha, exit by way of the lake's northern end. The mountain ridge that borders the lake's left shore dips low, providing easy access to the village of *Sallma* on the other side.

From Sallma, you cross the nearby stream and make your way to the opposite side of the valley a short distance below the village. Here the trail climbs the slope to a marshy pasture overlooking the valley. Continue along the left side of the pasture before climbing to the right of a rocky crag.

The pass lies just above 5050 meters and overlooks another broad valley. A lake can be seen on the far side of the valley. Descend to the left of the open area before you head to the valley below. Cross the rio *Chumayu* and climb toward the lake to where several houses stand nearby. Continue past the houses to a trail that runs along the slope above the lake. Take this trail over the spur of *Nv. Chuallani* which is on your right.

Standing on the spur, you look down into a basin of pasture land with a small pond. Above the pasture to the west, you can see the pass leading out of the region around Sibinacocha. The trail crosses the pasture below the pond, and then climbs steeply up the mountainside near Nv. Chuallani. This pass also lies at 5050 meters and takes an hour and a half to reach from the small lake.

The trail comes down from the pass through a long quebrada, and leads to the large valley of the *rio Chillcamayu* some three hours away. The trail remains high on the left slope of the quebrada, staying off its marshy floor. The trail is wide and the valley well populated with llamas and alpacas.

Huge herds of *llamas* and *alpacas* are tended throughout the Nv. Ausangate region. The domesticated members of the llamoid family share the highlands with their wild cousins the vicuña and the guanaco. A more distant relative, by some hundred thousand years of variant evolution, is the camel. Both llamoids and cameloids, linked by a common Eocene ancestor, share such characteristics as a split upper lip, two-toed feet, and an ability to store water in fats and carbohydrates. Llamas and alpacas differ from each other in that the llama is larger and has a longer neck than its cousin. The tail provides the easiest clue for differentiating the two: the llama's tail stands up while the alpaca's lies down flat over its rump.

Described by the conquistadores as a long-necked sheep, domesticated llamas have been present in Peruvian culture for three thousand years. Colonial law adopted an Incan edict forbidding the tending of herds by solitary men. Such fears of sodomy have bred the widely held misconception that this type of bestiality gave rise to the New World disease of syphilis.

Thriving best above 2500 meters, both llama and alpaca today provide highland campesinos with basic necessities. Primarily raised for its fine wool, the alpaca is shorn of its coat during the rainy season. Both animals' wool is used for clothing, and although the meat from the 400-pound llama does not compare to that of Old World livestock, it is still eaten. The Quechua word for sun-dried strips of llama meat is *charqui* (jerky), one of the few words of this Andean language to make it into English. Used as a pack animal, the llama can carry up to 100 pounds. Even the dung of the beasts is put to use and burned as fuel. The pellets are dried during the winter months and then stored in beehive-shaped stone-and-sod bins that are usually found near corrals and settlements.

You will pass some of these bins on your way down the quebrada as it nears the Chillcamayu. Camp in the quebrada just above their junction.

In the morning, you must choose between the trail to *Pitumarca* or the Ausangate-circuit trail to *Tinqui*. Both destinations can be reached in two or three days. If you decide to return to Pitumarca, stay to the left side of the quebrada. If you want to join the circuit trail at the upper end of the Chillcamayu, cross to the right side of the quebrada to enter the valley. The connection with the circuit trail lies two to two and a half hours up the valley next to several large corrals.

10

The Ausangate Short Circuit

ELEVATION GAIN: 600 m
ELEVATION LOSS: 600 m

LENGTH: 2-4 days
DISTANCE: 45 km

A hike along the northern face of the Ausangate massif provides some of the finest mountain scenery in the Cordillera Vilcanota, but it does not require long days of trekking nor the ascent of high passes. You can hike to two hot springs in as many days or include any number of side trips to lengthen your stay in the mountains. The Ausangate Short Circuit is flexible enough to match any level of hiking experience while still offering glacial ice, towering peaks, and many small villages to explore.

The Trek

Follow the directions for transportation and the first day of hiking as outlined in the Ausangate Circuit description. Camp above *Upis* and enjoy a refreshing bath in the shadow of the mountain.

On the second day return to Upis and follow the trail directly behind the village on the slope to the northeast. The trail passes a small chapel before reaching a plateau on the ridge and a group of houses. Continue along the trail that stays to the right and borders the steep slope of the ridge. The trail remains fairly level, reaching an elevation around 4600 meters, and begins to bend to the south back toward the mountain. After an hour and a half to two hours of hiking, you will reach a long, marshy pasture beneath a glacier and the main mountain face of Nv. Ausangate.

Horses graze in the pastures, and several hillocks offer fine campsites with a view. If you decide to make a short day of hiking and camp here, you can wander the ridges on either side of the pasture and enjoy some spectacular views. Toward Tinqui you can see another group of mountains, with *Nv. Jollyepunco* the tallest peak at 5522 meters. This range makes up the northern part of the Cordillera Vilcanota.

A more rigorous route to the pasture can be hiked from the hot springs above Upis by cutting over the ridge in an easterly direction. This route is considerably steeper but well worth the effort on a clear day, when Ausangate appears only a stone's throw away.

From the pasture, follow the trail past a single house and over a low spot in the eastern ridge. The overlook from the ridge provides a view of *Laguna Comercocha* directly to the east and backed by the peak of *Collque Cruz.* Several other small lakes can be seen at the head of the valley below the ridge.

You can now hike to Laguna Comercocha, where you can camp and then make a day hike to the ice cave at the pass before Qampa. Or you can follow the valley down to the hot springs near Pacchanta and then on to Tinqui. For more information on these routes see the description of the Ausangate Circuit.

The Cordillera Urubamba

North of the Sacred Valley of the Incas rises a range of mountains that takes its name from that valley's river. The Cordillera Urubamba is lower than its neighboring ranges, the Vilcanota and Vilcabamba. Its tallest peaks — Veronica, Chicon, Pitusiray, and Siwasiray — do not rise above 6000 meters. Although the mountains' grasp of the sky is not so lofty, this region has other virtues. The Cordillera Urubamba remains relatively unhiked by gringos, and its trails are not well-known.

For the adventurous trekker, the mountains and valleys of the range are ideal for exploration. Your explorations, however, will have to be carried on without the aid of IGM maps, which do not cover the region just north of the Sacred Valley. Instead, you will have to rely on road maps and other less-graphic charts. Trailheads into the cordillera can be found at almost all the towns and villages along the paved road of the Sacred Valley. Ollantaytambo, Yanahuara, Urubamba, Huaran, and Calca all have trails into the Cordillera Urubamba.

Many of these trails lead down into the high jungle valleys of *La Convencion.* These trails have quite ancient origins as the trade routes between the highland region around Cuzco and the upper jungles of the Amazon Basin. A road now runs into the jungle valleys from Calca, so you can plan on truck transport back to the Sacred Valley at the end of your hike.

While researching trails for this book, I hypothesized that some trail or system of trails must exist to the north of the mountain chain running parallel with the Sacred Valley to connect Calca with Ollantaytambo. My hypothesis proved true, but the path proved too difficult to include as a suggested route. The trek did, however, provide valuable, if hard-learned, lessons.

I left Calca and hiked above the road along an ancient and deteriorated trail. The trail had fallen away in places, so at times I was clutching at the mountainside and crawling along cliff ledges. This route taught me my first lesson. Always take a trail that has been in recent use, and do not take something with pre-Columbian potholes and vertical detours. At this point, I was still navigating by way of the IGM map entitled "Calca." I turned away from the road and headed up a quebrada to the lake of Mapacocha. There, with an ice-ladened mountain peak behind me, and geese and ducks making dusk landings on the lake, I set up camp.

The next day, I hiked to the mountain pass above the lake. Calling that low break in the mountain ridge a pass proved to be a bit of an overstatement. Instead, it was more a sandpile heaped high enough along the mountainside to provide access to the lowest jumble of rocks on the ridge. Large boulders had been piled in the notch of the ridge to prevent errant cows and sheep from straying to greener pastures beyond. Overcoming this barricade to lesser mammals, I took hopping strides down the steep sandpile on the other side to the valley below.

I had actually hopped right off the map: bounced myself into the unknown. My IGM map was of no use to me now, for it showed nothing but white paper. My gravity-propelled flight down the mountain took my mind off growing doubts as to my whereabouts and course. Without a good representative map of the area, I had to rely on poor maps and my own general notion of the area's geography. Both these navigational aids would have been useless, however, if I had not also brought along a compass, which I used to steer a northwesterly course. With a road map as my shield and a compass as my sword, I fought back all anxieties of going astray and forged ahead with a modicum of confidence. This was the second lesson learned about exploration: take whatever directional aids are available, including a compass.

I came to the small village of Cancha Cancha. The village spreads along the upper end of the valley that leads up from Huaran. I hiked past houses until I finally came to the village schoolhouse, where I met two teachers who were happy to have a visitor and to provide me with what information they could, most of which was extracted from the schoolchildren in Quechua and retold to me in Spanish.

The teacher's life in the rural districts is not an easy one. The rural teachers usually spend only a year or two in a village before they are promoted to a school in a larger town. Because of this, they are never fully integrated into the community, and remain outsiders. Neither is the teacher's job an easy one. In a country where over 40 percent of the population speaks Quechua as a first language, teaching is complicated by a need for bilingual instruction.

The conflict between the official language of Spanish and the widely used but largely unpublished language of Quechua has aggravated another problem — illiteracy. The national illiteracy rate in 1981 was 18 percent. In the mountains, where schooling is often inadequate or even inaccessible, illiteracy is much greater. In the Department of Cuzco, around 37 percent of those over fifteen years of age are illiterate, while in the neighboring Department of Apurimac, the rate is as high as 52 percent.

In Cancha Cancha, I was told that by heading up the valley and crossing a pass I could arrive in the valley of Lares. Instead, I chose a course that led over a different pass and on to the village of Concani. My path took me into a pasture with a natural amphitheater that had towering sides and a lacy waterfall cascading from the rim hundreds of meters above. A faint and winding trail led me up the side of this amphitheater. After reaching the amphitheater's rim, I walked a couple hundred meters to a lake cradled beneath the mountain peak of Puncu Puncu, and here I made camp.

Dead branches from squat and twisted trees littered the ground and provided a rare opportunity for a campfire. That night, before the wind-whipped flames, my mind was drawn back to ghost tales told in my youth around similar fires. Thoughts of these childhood phantoms mixed with thoughts of the apus and soqas that I'd heard about while living in Cuzco. I then recalled what one of the teachers had told me as he led me up into the pasture of the amphitheater that afternoon. Years before, a couple of gringos had visited Cancha Cancha with the intention of climbing the nearby mountain of Colque Cruz. Colque Cruz means Silver Cross, and it is believed that the peak hides such a precious object. The true objective of the climbers was this cross, said the teacher. The climbers started their ascent, but as they neared the peak, the campesinos below heard a loud crack ring out from the mountain. They saw the climber in the lead fall down the mountain, the top of his skull cleanly cut away. The teacher just looked at me and said not another word after relating this gruesome tale.

Stories of freakish death in the mountains are not uncommon in the Andes. Although my companion made no mention of supernatural forces, the malevolent actions of an apu were clearly implied. General belief among campesinos holds that to climb a mountain is to tempt the anger of mountain spirits and to court disaster. Since local people have no desire to anger the spirits, gringos with their fetish for climbing mountains often become the victims of vengeful apus in these tales.

Solitude is easily found in the Cordillera Urubamba.

In some areas, it is even believed that each year an apu will take a certain number of lives as sacrifices. Therefore, you can expect little help from the locals if a member of your party is injured on a mountain. They believe it is the will of the apu, and aiding the injured will only expose them to the danger of his supernatural wrath.

These thoughts still drifted through my mind as I went to sleep that night. The next morning, I awoke to foul weather and a light dusting of snow on the ground. Marshy ground and broken stone covered the distance between the camp and pass, and without any evidence of a trail I was forced to carefully pick my way up the slope. At the pass I came face to face both with snow and rain blowing from the northwest and with the realization of my third lesson of exploration: never hike alone.

Visibility had reduced to no more than thirty meters as I skittered down the large, loose rock that made up the other side of the pass. I often looked in the direction of the cloud-shrouded peaks, wondering if some malevolent apu was planning *my* untimely demise. With painstaking and lonesome steps, I at last reached the more secure ground of the valley below.

The next several days of hiking revealed less difficult trail as I walked through the villages of Concani, Huacawasi, and Huilloc before finally ending my trek at Ollantaytambo. Although the weather never permitted an unobstructed view of the region's peaks, the valleys were spectacular in their beauty and isolation from the roads and towns of the Sacred Valley.

11

Ollantaytambo to Ccachin
Weavers Trek

ELEVATION GAIN: 1482 m   LENGTH: 4-5 days
ELEVATION LOSS: 1750 m   DISTANCE: 58 km

The Cordillera Urubamba and its surrounding valleys are the home of some of the finest weavers in South America. Employing techniques dating back thousands of years, the women of Ccachin and Cochayoc spin, dye, and weave wool into *mantas,* shawls, of intricate designs. You can meet the weavers and purchase their handiworks as you trek through the valleys. The campesinos of the villages greet visitors warmly, offering their brand of Andean hospitality. This route was first run by Tambo Treks of Ollantaytambo.

How to Get There
To arrive at Ollantaytambo, either take a train from the San Pedro station or take a minibus from Av. Huascar 128 to Urubamba, and then continue on by small truck or van to the Inca townsite.

The Trek
Horses for the trek can be found in Huilloc, a three-and-a-half- to four-hour walk above Ollanta. By asking around in the

village, you can find a horse and *arriero,* horseman, for around US $3 a day.

Begin in Ollanta by following the road that runs up along the waters of the *Patacancha* from between the two plazas. The road crosses the stream several times before finally remaining on the right bank till Huilloc. The left slope of the valley has been heavily terraced and now lies mostly unattended. After one and a half to two hours' walking, you'll come to the confluence of the Patacancha and *Yuramayu.* You can see on the ridge opposite the road the ruins of Pumamarca, a defensive structure left by the Incas.

At a waterfall in the stream, a trail cuts up the valleyside as the road switchbacks up the slope. As you climb above the waterfall, more Inca ruins can be seen in the valley and along the slopes.

After hiking three and a half to four hours, you will reach the village of *Huilloc.* This community provides a large number of the porters and cooks working on the Inca Trail, so consequently the villagers are accustomed to gringos and their rather odd habits. You can camp in the field in front of the school or continue on to *Patacancha,* less than two hours away.

As you leave Huilloc, stay on the trail along the right bank of the stream, where halfway to Patacancha you'll meet the road again. At this writing, the road stops just short of the village of Patacancha, at which point you cross the stream. You can camp at the schoolyard or continue another thirty minutes up the valley to a pampa to camp.

The night we camped at Patacancha we squeezed everything into a small two-man tent. Everything, that is, except the horse, which hardly seemed practicable. At 1:00 a.m. Nicanor, the arriero, awoke to find his horse gone. He set out in search of his stallion while I ungallantly fell back asleep.

It wasn't until 10:30 the next morning that I saw Nicanor again. He arrived with a harried look on his face, one fagged horse, and a tale of horse thieving in the high mountains.

At around 11:00 the night before, a band of horse thieves had moved up the valley, adding one more horse to their already considerable lot as they passed our camp. Nicanor literally headed the thieves off at the pass, catching up with them around 3 a.m. at the Abra de Kelcanca, where the bandits were enjoying shots of aquardiente (the drink of choice among *bandidos*) to fend off the night's chill. Words were exchanged. A scuffle ensued and Nicanor's *chullo,* wool cap, was torn but he himself left unharmed. The bandits finally relented, figuring it better to lose a horse than kill a man. They returned the horse and rather politely asked to be excused of their indiscretion.

Nicanor then descended to his home in Kelcanca on the other side of the pass before returning to Patacancha by daylight. When the three of us finally arrived in Kelcanca that evening, Nicanor and the horse had been over the route three times in less than fifteen hours.

From Patacancha the *Abra de Kelcanca* lies some three and a half to four hours away. Continue following the stream via the trail along its left bank. The trail climbs through a series of rises before reaching a broad, marshy pampa. Here cross the stream to the right and stay above the marshy ground, making your way along the slope. On the pampa and along the slopes Andean geese may be seen. The trail often disappears as it heads for the pass but becomes distinct again as it climbs the last few hills to the Abra de Kelcanca. The abra is a low opening in the hills, probably not much over 4000 meters in elevation.

The trail heads off the pass to the right over rolling hills. Follow the trail down as it bends to the right, and after some forty-five minutes to an hour you'll reach the first houses of Kelcanca—small huts on the right side of the valley and a house with a corral on the left. Here the trail crosses to the left side of the valley and continues its descent. Once you reach

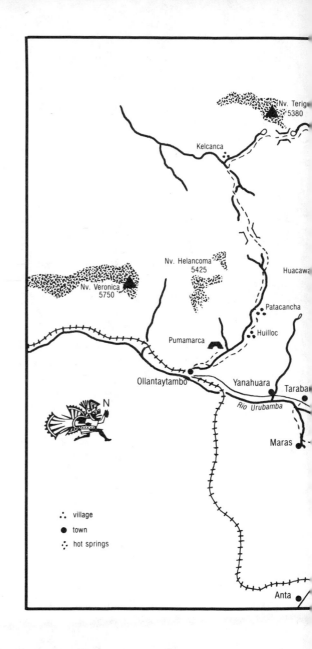

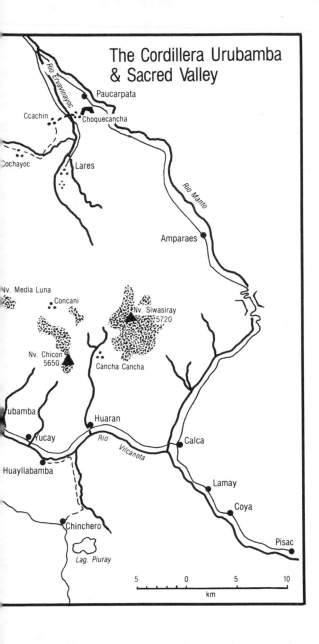

The Cordillera Urubamba & Sacred Valley

Rio Ervavinayoc

Paucarpata

Ccachin

Choquecancha

Cochayoc

Lares

Rio Manto

Amparaes

Nv. Media Luna

Concani

Nv. Siwasiray
5720

Nv. Chicon
5650

Cancha Cancha

Urubamba

Huaran

Yucay

Rio Vilcanota

Calca

Huayllabamba

Lamay

Coya

Chinchero

Lag. Piuray

Pisac

5   0   5   10

km

the junction of two valleys, follow the trail to the left into the new valley until you reach an open area beside the stream more than an hour from the pass. Camp here for the night.

Continuing downstream the next day, you'll soon come to a group of houses and corrals along the right bank. At the lower end of this settlement, jump the stream to the right bank and head down-valley to where you enter yet another broad valley, at the bottom of which is nestled the main village of Kelcanca. You can descend to the village for a closer look or stay high on the mountainside to begin your ascent of the final pass.

In the distance you can see a group of mountains known as the *Teriguays*, considered by some people to be a northern mountain group distinct from the Cordillera Urubamba. The Teriguays' tallest peak reaches a height of 5380 meters.

The *Abra de Yanacocha*, at the southern extreme of the mountains, lies some three hours from Kelcanca. The trail, winding past houses, fields, and corrals, stays to the right side of the valley and climbs gently to just beneath the mountains. From here it steepens and passes the small lake of *Yuracocha*, White Lake, beyond which an upper meadow offers good camping. The final climb to the abra takes you to a height of 4250 meters.

From the pass follow the trail to the right around *Yanacocha*, Black Lake, and descend to a broad valley below. *Cochayoc* lies some two to two and a half hours from the abra. The trail runs past the burnt-orange cliffs and shale of Pucaorco, Red Mountain, and on to the village. Campsites can be found in one of the fields just below the main village or just off the trail beside the church.

Unlike the other side of the pass, the valley around Cochayoc supports a relative abundance of trees. The houses, with their extended awnings and side walls forming a type of porch unique to the region, remind me of the three-sided buildings found at Machu Picchu. The weavers of Cochayoc, the equal

Weaving is a daily part of village life in Cochayoc.

of those in Ccachin, are happy to demonstrate their craft for you and sell what mantas (sometimes called *llicllas*) they have on hand. In exchange for a demonstration or picture, it is often appropriate to give something in return, such as school supplies or food. Money should only be used to purchase mantas and should be in Peruvian currency, not dollars. Prices vary from US $20 to $30 (depending on the quality of the work) and are open to bargaining.

Ccachin lies another two and a half to three hours down the trail. Continue down-valley, entering a narrow ravine where you ford the stream a half hour out of Cochayoc, and then begin a gradual ascent as the stream falls away below. The drop from the trail's edge is steep and spectacular, and as you head northeast *Nv. Siwasiray* (5720 meters) comes into view. The trail gradually rounds to the left and Ccachin stands perched on the slope below. Descend toward Ccachin and camp at the water tank, a low block structure just above the village.

Ccachin is a beautiful village of thatch-roofed houses, flowering trees and shrubs, and hospitable people. Nearly all the women weave, beginning at the age of 6 or 7 by spinning wool and a year or so later taking up the backstrap loom. Hundreds of hours of work go into the hand-woven mantas known for their intricate and numerous designs. One design shows the eighteenth-century rebel Tupac Amaru II pulled from each limb by horses in an unsuccessful attempt to tear him apart.

Trucks pass along the road below Ccachin between 7 and 10 o'clock each morning. To descend to the road, take one of the trails down out of Ccachin, joining the main trail below the face of the bluff. With good knees, the steep, jarring hike down takes about an hour. If no trucks pass in the morning, you can either hike down along the road to where it joins the main road some two hours away, or you can climb to the town and Inca ruins of Choquecancha and take the wide trail that cuts across and over the ridge to Paucarpata on the main road. Truck traffic is more frequent along the main road but still unscheduled.

Manu National Park

Southeast of Cuzco the mountains drop away like a seawall to an ocean of clouds below, where lies one of the last vestiges of an untouched jungle wilderness in the Amazon Basin. Here, in the Biosphere Reserve of Manu, toucans, jaguars, spider monkeys, and giant otters survive in the green density of the jungle just as they have done for hundreds of years. Saved by its remoteness from the encroachments of man, the immense park contains a diversity of virgin ecosystems.

Truly immense in its proportions, Manu's borders enclose an area the size of Massachusetts, and is the third-largest national park on the continent. Some four and a half million acres in all, the park and its reserve lands stretch from the desolate highlands of the Department of Cuzco to the lush jungle lowlands of the Madre de Dios. Because of the park's diverse lands, Manu contains a staggering array of flora and fauna.

An uncatalogued multitude of flowering plants (the estimates range from two thousand to five thousand species) flourish in the park, brightening everything from its mountainsides to its lowlands. Macaws and prehistoric hoatzins, harkening from a distant age, share the skies, trees, and waterways with another eight hundred species of bird. The park also serves as a living museum for many of the world's near-extinct species: ocelots drink from the rio Manu's slow-moving waters, and giant otters, some as large as two meters long, play and hunt in oxbow lakes. South America's largest animal, the tapir, hides in the dense jungle foliage; the green wall of trees also provides a home for thirteen species of monkeys. The rivers and lakes of the region support docile and not-so-docile aquatic life. Resting on logs floating atop the water, a row of sleepy river turtles often lie piggy-back against each other, while beneath the rivers' brown waters, black caimans (South America's crocodile) and grinning piranhas lurk.

Geography & Climate

Starting from the mountainous region beyond Paucartambo, the lands of the Manu National Park and its adjacent Reserved Zone drop from 4000 meters to a tenth of that elevation northwest of Puerto Maldonado in the Amazon Basin. The park encompasses the watershed of the 250-kilometer-long rio Manu, which flows into the rio Madre de Dios outside the park boundaries. Both rivers compose just a miniscule portion of the water in the vast Amazon Basin.

The tropical climate of the jungle region around the rio Manu follows seasonal changes found higher in the Andes. The rainy season stretches from October to May and is the time in which much of the park's two meters of annual rainfall occurs. During the rainy season, the road leading into the park can become impassable, and the swollen Alto Madre de Dios becomes treacherous. From June to September, the dry season often offers rainless periods lasting several weeks. Temperatures in the dry season range from 28° to 32°C. (81° to 90°F.), with temperatures at night dipping to around 20° to 26°C. (68° to 79°F.).

Tourism

The isolation and remoteness of the rio Manu has left the surrounding region nearly untouched by man. Scientists recognized the uniqueness of the region in the late sixties, but it was not until 1973 that the Peruvian government awarded it national-park status. Then, in 1977, the park won further protection when UNESCO made it a biosphere reserve by declaring it the representative of one of the world's major ecosystems.

Because the park is still young, tourism remains in its infancy. The few facilities that exist are crude and rugged, but they offer excellent possibilities for viewing the park's flora and fauna. The areas around two oxbow lakes have recently been cleared for camping, and a system of well-marked trails connects these lakes with the river. At each of the lakes, wooden canoes are available for tourists' use. No lodges, tents, cooking facilities, or food are available within the park. In the true form of exploration, all necessary supplies must be brought into the park and, when leaving, the explorers must carry their garbage out. A small fee is charged for daily use of the park.

Medical Precautions

A full set of immunizations as outlined in the introductory section should be received before entering the park. Malaria doesn't exist in the park itself, but malarial areas do exist outside the park. As a precaution, anti-malaria drugs should be taken as prescribed.

Drinking the water from the rio Manu is most likely safe, though the same cannot be said for the Alto Madre de Dios, which drains many of the highland areas around Cuzco. To be safe, you should not drink any untreated water.

Travel to the Park

Manu's isolation has made it the special wilderness it is, but it has also made it difficult and very expensive to reach. For those people with enough time and money to make the journey on their own, I have included several methods of reaching the park. I am indebted to the park management for the following information, as I am for much of the above information.

You can avail yourself of two travel methods to reach Manu National Park. Either a combination of travel by road and river or a combination of travel by air and river will bring you to the rio Manu.

You start a trip by road and river in Cuzco by traveling overland on 257 kilometers of rough dirt road to *Shintuya*. Several trucks run the route and charge between $15 and $25. The trip takes from one to three days, depending on the vehicle and road conditions.

At Shintuya you need to find a boat and competent boatman to take you down the rough waters of the Alto Madre de Dios. The four- to six-hour journey will bring you to the *Boca de Manu,* where the Manu meets the Alto Madre de Dios. Good boatmen and boats are not easy to come by and can run as much as $150 to $300 a day. The park management suggests booking a boatman months in advance by writing to them at Casilla 1057, Cuzco, Peru. Otherwise, you can expect to spend considerable time in Shintuya looking for transport.

The second method of reaching the park, by air and river, is considerably faster and more comfortable, but also a great deal more expensive. Start by taking a commercial jet flight to *Puerto Maldonado* for $40. You should arrange several weeks in advance to take a charter flight with Aerocondor from Pt. Maldonado to *Boca Manu.* The flight takes around sixty minutes and costs around $270 to $300 per hour. If the plane flies back empty, you will, of course, pay for that, too. You will need to have arranged for a boat to meet you at the park entrance to take you upriver into the park and to the camp areas.

If all this sounds incredibly expensive and troublesome, it is, and the alternative is to take a packaged tour into the park. Currently, only one company in Cuzco runs tours into the park on short notice. *Expediciones Manu* runs seven- and nine-day trips into the park for around $500. Trips leave on the first Sunday of every month from April to November. Run by Hugo Pepper, their offices can be found at Procuradores 50. Other companies run trips into the park but usually require bookings well in advance.

Appendix A
Trilingual Guide

When hiking in the country, you will find that knowing just a little Spanish goes a long way. Quechua, however, is the first and perhaps only language of the majority of campesinos. In fact, 40 percent of the present population of Peru speaks Quechua as a first language.

Unlike many conquered peoples' languages, the Incan language did not succumb to the victor's tongue. Instead, Quechua, a language the Incas adopted from a tribe near Abancay, was in turn adopted by the Spanish and used in particular situations. The conquerors propagated Quechua throughout the old empire, so that it actually increased in usage and spread beyond its old borders. Only recently has the Quechua language begun to decline in usage.

In some of the more remote areas, particularly around Ausangate, the campesinos' ability to speak Spanish is practically nonexistent. Once when I asked an old man how far it was to the pass, he replied most emphatically, "Es muy caro." ("It's very expensive.") In hindsight, this irrelevant answer nearly proved correct. After crossing the ridge in a flurry of snow and hail, I almost paid with my life descending the steep, slippery slope.

When you need to ask directions, try to phrase your questions so as to require a definite answer. Perhaps because they are so eager to please, or maybe in a holdover from the time of the Conquest when anything was said to rid themselves of the invaders, campesinos will invariably answer, given a yes/ no question, with what you want to hear. Even when you do get a detailed reply, the information may still not fit the situation, the reason being the campesino, who may spend his entire life in the confines of a few mountain valleys, has a different concept of time and space. His relation to the environment has little to do with watches and measured distance, so you may be told a place is quite near when in fact it takes a day to reach.

You may find the following list of words and phrases useful in the countryside. The Quechua words and phrases follow Spanish spellings and pronunciations, hence *ll* is pronounced like the English *y* in *you,* and *cc* has a deep guttural sound like a coughed-up *q.*

Phrases

English	*Spanish*	*Quechua*
Hello	Hola	Alabado (Praise God)
How are you?	¿Como estás?	Allinllachu kasianqui?
I'm fine.	Estoy bien.	Allillanmi kasiani.
What is your name?	¿Como se llama?	Iman sutiqui?
My name is. . .	Me llamo. . .	Nuccac suticca. . .
good-bye	adios/ciao	uc cuti coma
Where is. . .?	¿Donde está. . .?	Maipi. . .?
Where is water?	¿Donde está el agua?	Maipin unu casian?
Where is the path to. . .?	¿Donde está el camino a. . .?	Maipin. . .ñan?
Can we camp here?	¿Podemos campar aqui?	Atisun manchu samaita caipi?
What is the name of that. . .?	¿Como se llama ese. . .?	Imatac sutin accai. . .?
Where are you walking?	¿A donde está camianado?	Maitan purishianqui?
I'm walking to. . .	Estoy caminando a. . .	Purishani. . .
I want. . .	yo quiero. . .	munani. . .

Vocabulary

English	Spanish	Quechua
what	que	ima
who	quien	pi
where	donde	may
which	cual	maikan
yes/no	si/no	ari/mana
water	agua	unu
food	comida	mihuna
wind	viento	huayra
fire	fuego	nina
snow	nieve	riti
path	camino/sendero	ñan
river	rio	mayu
stream	quebrada	wayqo
field	campo	pampa
mountain	montaña	orqo
hill	cerro	orqo
lake	laguna	cocha
village	pueblo	llaqta
house	casa	wasi
good/bad	bueno/malo	allin/mana allin
hot/cold	calor/frio	rupay/chiri
left/right	izquierda/derecha	lloque/paña
near/far	cerca/lejos	sispa/karu
big/small	grande/pequeño	hatun/huchuy

Appendix B
The Legend of Inkarrí

Born in the days that followed the Conquest, the legend of Inkarrí still exists today. Several versions of the legend circulate throughout southern Peru, but amid the confusion caused by varying details certain common ideas and motifs shine through. The legend depicts Inkarrí as the embodiment of both the creator-god Viracocha and the powerful lord Inca. When the Spanish came to the Andes, they tricked and killed him. Now, the awaited resurrection and return of Inkarrí foreshadows a new world for the campesinos — the completion of an Andean nation interrupted by the invasion of the Spanish.

The Sun and the Moon gave birth to Inkarrí, who was given complete power over the world. At his command, stones walked. With his strength, he "tied" his father the Sun down so as to make the days longer. Through his powers, he put the natural world in order and also civilized its inhabitants.

Then, his brother, referred to in the different versions of the legend as Espanarrí, el Presidente, or even Jesus Christ, became quite envious of Inkarri and murdered him by cutting off his head. Inkarrí's body was buried in the Andean soil, but his head was hidden away.

Although Inkarrí's head and body were separated centuries ago, over the many years they both have been growing toward each other in an effort to reunite. This day is close at hand. When they are once again united, Inkarrí shall rise up to expel the foreigners from his lands and to complete the work he set out long ago to perform — the ordering and civilizing of his Andean world.

Bibliography

Angles Vargas, Vitor. *Historia del Cuzco;*
Industrial grafica S.A.; Lima, Peru; 1978.

Frost, Peter. *Exploring Cuzco;*
Bradt Ent.; Bucks, England; 1984.

Gasparini, Graziana & Luise Margolies. *Arquitectura Inka;*
Universidad Central de Venezuela; Caracas, Venezuela;
1977.

Hackett, Peter. *Mountain Sickness;*
American Alpine Club; NY, USA; 1980.

Hemming, John. *The Conquest of the Incas;*
Penguin Books; New York, USA; 1983.

Hemming, John & Edward Ranney. *Monuments of the Incas;*
Little, Brown, & Co.; Boston, USA; 1982.

Kendall, Ann. *Everyday Life of the Incas;*
Batsford, Ltd.; London, England; 1973.

Meisch, Lynn. *A Traveler's Guide to El Dorado
& the Inca Empire;*
Penguin Books; New York, USA; 1977.

Morrison, Tony. *Land Above the Clouds;*
The Trinity Press; London, England; 1974.

Protzen, Jean-Pierre. "Inca Stonemasonry,"
Scientific American; Feb. 1986; Vol. 254:2.

Von Hagen, Victor. *Realm of the Incas;*
New York, USA; 1957.

Index

Andes
  geography 3-5
  name 7
  people 5-6
Animals
  general 31
  Andean goose 89
  Andean gull 120-121
  coati 115
  condor 103-105
  giant coot 138
  hummingbird 103
  llama 31, 140-142
  mountain caracara 124
  mountain viscacha 127
  pack animals 11
  torrent duck 132
  vicuna 137-138
Apu 34, 118, 121, 148, 150
Aywar Fiesta 105
Chicha 41
Coca 115-116
Equipment 8-12
Food 12-13
Garbage 32
High Altitude Sickness 18-19
Hypothermia 20
Inca
  agriculture 60-61, 76-77
  empire 6-7, 48-49
  messengers 53
  roads 53, 81-82
  stone masonry 94-95
Maps vi, 14, 45, 79, 100-101, 122-123, 154-155
Metric Conversions 16
Pachamama 33-34

Potato 130-131, 136
Quechua
  language 164-166
  people 28-30, 131
Robbery 26, 27-28
Ruins
  general 31
  Cachiqata 94
  Choquetacca 95
  Huchuy Qosqo 55, 56-57
  Huinay Huiyna 83
  Llactapata 76-77
  Machu Picchu 85
  Maucallacta 69-70
  Palcay 114
  Paucarcancha 90, 107
  Phuyupatamarca 81-83
  Puca Pucara 41
  Pumamarca 61, 152
  Puma Orqo 70
  Qenco 41
  Runkuracay 78
  Sacsayhuaman 40-41
  Sayajmarca 78, 80-81
  Tambomachay 41-42
  Tampu Toco 71
Sacred Objects 34-35, 50, 68, 110
Sacred Valley 22-23
South American Explorers
  Club 14-15
Sun Stroke 20
Trails 26-27
Trains 22, 25-26
Trucks 23-25
Water 21
Weather 7-8